LOOKING FOR **ANDY GRIFFITH**

EVAN DALTON SMITH

LOOKING

FOR

ANDY

GRIFFITH

A FATHER'S JOURNEY

The University of North Carolina Press
CHAPEL HILL

This book was published with the assistance of the Blythe Family Fund of the University of North Carolina Press.

Manufactured in the United States of America
Designed and typeset by Lindsay Starr
Set in Sentinel

Cover art: (left) courtesy of the author and (right) courtesy of UNC–Chapel Hill Department of Dramatic Art Photographs and Related Materials, Wilson Special Collections Library, UNC–Chapel Hill.

LIBRARY OF CONGRESS CATALOGING-IN-PUBLICATION DATA

Names: Smith, Evan Dalton, author.
Title: Looking for Andy Griffith / Evan Dalton Smith.
Description: Chapel Hill : The University of North Carolina Press, [2024] | Includes bibliographical references and index.
Identifiers: LCCN 2023044349 | ISBN 9781469678986 (cloth) | ISBN 9781469678993 (epub) | ISBN 9798890887498 (pdf)
Subjects: LCSH: Griffith, Andy, 1926–2012. | Smith, Evan Dalton. | Actors—North Carolina—Biography. | North Carolina—Biography. | BISAC: BIOGRAPHY & AUTOBIOGRAPHY / Entertainment & Performing Arts | LITERARY CRITICISM / American / General | LCGFT: Creative nonfiction. | Biographies. | Autobiographies.
Classification: LCC PN2287.G69 S65 2024 | DDC 792.02/8092 [B]— dc23/eng/20231019
LC record available at https://lccn.loc.gov/2023044349

FOR MY CHILDREN, COLEMAN DALTON AND
REBECCA PEARL, AND MY MOM AND DAD,
BETTY JEAN AND BOBBY LEE

CONTENTS

A section of illustrations begins on page 91.

WE ALL THINK WE ESCAPE AND THEN SPEND
THE REST OF OUR LIVES WRITING ABOUT
OUR PRISONS.

—Mary Lee Settle

An Ideal Program
for every group and budget

Andy and Barbara Griffith offer one of the most unusual and entertaining programs to be found today. Their act is as versatile as it is warm and appealing to every type of audience.

Both natives of North Carolina. Andy graduated from U.N.C. with a degree in music. His wife Barbara is a music major from Converse College. Both of them have had considerable acting, dancing and singing experience and have gained a large following through their appearance in Paul Green's THE LOST COLONY as Sir Walter Raleigh and Eleanor Dare.

Their Program:

SINGING . . . Barbara Griffith's lovely, dramatic soprano voice is heard in a wide range of selections including operatic, light opera, folk ballad and popular.

COMEDY CHARACTER SKETCHES . . . Andy Griffith's comic characters have brought him acclaim across the state as the best in rural humor. Similar to Will Rogers in their warmth and simplicity, they include The Country Drummer, The Backwoods Deacon and The Guest Lecturer who speaks on every subject from Modern Song and Book Reviews to illustrated talks on any given topic.

INTERPRETIVE DANCES . . . Barbara Griffith has created a group of dances that interpret the lyrics and mood of Early American folk ballads as played on the guitar and sung by her husband.

DRAMATIC READINGS . . . The young couple join together to bring you famous scenes from great plays like ELIZABETH THE QUEEN and SALOME, as well as modern comedy sketches.

VAUDEVILLE . . . A medley of songs and dances from the 30's that features the Griffiths in the costumes and antics of the period. A nostalgic touch of the old vaudeville that we all love so well.

The Griffiths Are Prepared To Bring Your Group Any Size Or Length Program You Desire. Their Team Can Be Enlarged To A Company Of Ten Excellent Entertainers.

Each Program Patterned To Your Needs

Barbara and Andy Griffith as they appeared on the cover of THE LOST COLONY program.

Andy Griffith in one of his many rural character interpretations.

Barbara Griffith has received wide acclaim for her singing and acting ability.

Andy and Barbara interpret ballads with dance and song.

ANDY AND BARBARA GRIFFITH OFFER ONE OF THE MOST UNUSUAL AND ENTERTAINING PROGRAMS TO BE FOUND TODAY. THEIR ACT IS AS VERSATILE AS IT IS WARM AND APPEALING TO EVERY TYPE OF AUDIENCE.

—from Andy and Barbara's promotional brochure

A trifold brochure created by Andy and Barbara to promote show bookings. The brochure was mailed to civic groups, social clubs, and other organizations in the region when Andy and Barbara decided to make a go of it in the entertainment industry. Andy borrowed $1,000 from civic leaders Robert Smith and James Yokley—his father's employer at the Mount Airy Chair Company—to pay for the brochure.

The brochure's interior. Notice that Andy's "comedy character sketches" is one of five listed offerings in the program, with Barbara's singing at the top.

LOOKING FOR ANDY GRIFFITH

INT. CONVERTED BARN, MOUNT AIRY, NC—DAY

There's an infant asleep in a dresser drawer. Dovetailed, with a walnut veneer, the dresser is inlaid with a lighter maple. Its maker crafted the interiors with white pine. It's eighty-six years old, made in 1840 by the skilled hands of the infant's great-grandmother's brother, who lived and died in the hollows of the Virginia mountains. It's a solid piece of furniture but not intended for a sleeping baby.

The young parents of the infant, Geneva and Carl Lee, are living with their relatives in a converted barn, contributing fifteen dollars a month for room and board, until they can afford their own home and maybe pay for a crib—a store-bought crib with white lacquer and a sliding rail, ordered from the Spiegel catalog, or maybe from a second-hand store off Main Street, in Mount Airy, North Carolina.

EXT. SANDY BEACH—DAY

At an abandoned military base on North Carolina's Roanoke Island—a green oasis of native grasses, coral honeysuckle, and wild indigo in the waters between the brackish lowlands and the sand-blown string of barrier islands known as the Outer Banks—a group of young men and women amble about the beach. They're fit and tan, good-looking, all in their early twenties, lounging in cutoff shorts and bathing suits. It's the summer of 1947. Only a few years earlier, the remains of drowned sailors, their ships sunk by German submarines, washed ashore nearby on Hatteras and Ocracoke. Across the Atlantic, Europe still smolders, while the people of the United States have redirected their wartime energies to matters of industry, education, and entertainment.

A young man with a shock of thick, wavy brown hair sits on his long haunches and strums a guitar, a cigarette dangling from the corner of his mouth. His eyes are trained on a regal young woman as she sings the last few notes of an aria, Mozart's "Ruhe Sanft," in which the heroine Zaide rescues her lover, Gomatz. Friends listen nearby, sitting cross-legged and sipping cans of beer. Another group about twenty yards away is roping off a volleyball court in the sand. These young people have the entirety of the place, the mud-colored beach, the massive base—its acres are for their use alone—as if they are the only spirits on earth. A school bus will arrive to ferry them the few miles to the Waterside Theater at the Fort Raleigh National Historic Site, but that won't happen for hours. The guitar player transitions to a tune by Huddie Ledbetter (otherwise known as Lead Belly), whose folk-blues record they'd been listening to late into the night at the base canteen. The young man is Andy Griffith. He sings "House of the Rising Sun" in a full-throated baritone rather than imitate Lead Belly's famous tenor.

Turning from the volleyball game, Andy's good friend Bob—an Alabama native with gleaming dark eyes who'd escaped Birmingham's steel mills to study the dramatic arts as a Carolina Playmaker—cups thick hands over his mouth and shouts, "I love it. Sing louder, Andy!" Andy flashes a huge smile, glad he sacrificed summer wages to be there. Rather than work on the factory floor at the furniture plant with his father as he did in previous years, he's a player in the cast of *The Lost Colony*. The job pays half as much as he'd have earned if he'd stayed home, but there are obvious perks, including room and board, and the beer at the canteen is kept ice cold. The costumes are stifling, the physicality exhausting, but each day is invigorating—there's pure joy in the making. And with everyone living, working, and playing together all day, all summer—life, work, and fun blended as one—it's the best thing Andy's experienced. Choosing to take a cut in pay is the most profound impractical decision of his life.

INT. ALVIN THEATER, NYC—NIGHT

The performance that night was off, Andy thought; why couldn't they have come on a better night? It was a Wednesday, and the theater wasn't entirely full. There were a few biggish laughs and applause at the end, but the laughs weren't everywhere they were supposed to be and there was no standing ovation. Andy thought of how a few years back he stood over that skinny kid in the office above the music store in Greensboro, with his sound equipment, twisting the knobs, cutting tape, and tweaking the laughter, splicing it, until it was everywhere it was needed. The laughs for the "Romeo and Juliet" monologue were spliced at the end of the football bit.

"The show was off, Dick."

"You hit all the marks—all your lines. The show was perfect," Andy's manager said.

"It was off." Andy shook his head and grabbed the back of his neck, as if he was testing to see if he could wrench his head off.

"Why on a Wednesday? This is the third damn time they watched me perform."

"Let's get over there," Dick said.

"They're already at the table. We'll slide out the front to save steps."

As Dick and Andy walked the dozen or so paces east past the brick and stone facade of the Alvin Theatre on Fifty-Second Street, in the bright night of Manhattan's Theater District, Dick said to Andy, "Budd thinks you might be too nice to play it. Don't be too nice."

"Not a problem at all," Andy said.

This meeting was their last shot. Elia Kazan had been circling Andy for weeks. He'd seen him onstage. They'd met in Shubert Alley. The role was the lead in the great director's follow-up to *On the Waterfront*, which came out the year before, 1954. This new film was based on Budd Schulberg's short story "Your Arkansas Traveler." The hesitancy wasn't so much that Andy didn't have enough charisma, star power—he did. He lit up a room. He had energy about him. The concern was that maybe Andy couldn't play dark enough, couldn't be vicious, cynical, and devilish. Andy knew this was their fear. So he'd show them charisma—and he'd give them the devil.

Andy's hands were not the hands of a typical actor. They were not soft or weak. He could break your hand when he shook it if he wanted. Andy's hands were chafed and callused—a workingman's hands, and on top of that, a working musician's hands. They'd sawed timber, hammered nails, reached under the hood of more cars than one could count, shoveled dirt, loaded shotguns, gutted fish, and played every musical instrument until his fingers bled. His hands were large, oversize, and strong. And by the end of the meeting at the red leather banquette in the back corner of the restaurant, Andy had gripped Elia Kazan's skull in his hands, from both sides, and stood over him and preached like an old-time circuit rider, like a healing evangelist. Kazan's eyes bulged out wide. Andy felt the electric current passing between them and everyone at the table, everyone at Gallaghers Steakhouse late that night, watching Andy. All eyes were on him. Andy landed the part.

EXT. SWIMMING POOL — DAY

CLOSE on a gnawed pencil. A bright orange Ticonderoga no. 2, six inches long, marred by compressions left by teeth, set firmly within the wet mouth of Andy Griffith, as he floats on the rippling blue water.

ALL ART CONSTANTLY ASPIRES TOWARDS
THE CONDITION OF MUSIC.

—Walter Pater

1.

Ravaged by Alzheimer's, my father—whom I never once met—somehow had the wherewithal to starve himself.

2.

In the early 1930s, Roanoke Island, North Carolina, was a remote and hardscrabble place, sparsely populated with a few thousand people, mostly descended from a handful of families who raked out hard lives, fishing the waters, battling storms, and farming land for the better part of a few hundred years. Exactly when they arrived is mostly lost and debated. For decades in Manteo, the county seat of Dare County, locals had marked the occasion of Virginia Dare's birth; some read poems and children sang, sometimes dressed in period costume. The yearly event grew in popularity and gained the attention of the newspapers. Someone had the idea to ask Paul Green to write something to commemorate the birth of Virginia Dare and the Roanoke settlement. A Pulitzer Prize–winning playwright, Green left New York City after a successful career writing for the stage and moved back to his native North Carolina. In the trade publications of the day his NYC peers lampooned Green for his heavy southern accent.

(One would think lampooning people over their accent is a relic of a different era, but the contemporary writer Bronwen Dickey, who was raised in South Carolina and went to high school in Connecticut and to college at Duke, told me that when she was in graduate school at Columbia, from 2005 to 2007, populated mostly by a northeastern elite set, her classmates, after hearing she was southern, assumed she was stupid. "I noticed the surprise in their faces when I said I'd read James Wood's literary criticism." I experienced the same, at that same institution, compounded by the fact that I am large and affable and a bit of a slow talker. It seemed I was the sole person in my class who'd gone to a public university for my undergraduate degree. One classmate pointedly asked me if anyone in my family was in the Klan.)

Paul Green moved back to North Carolina not so much fleeing New York but for a plum teaching position at the University of North Carolina alongside his old professor Mr. Koch, who'd started the Playmakers program, which Green had joined as a student, writing folk plays. As a young man, Green had written a play that intimated what had happened to the English colony at Roanoke, where it had been abandoned. It was called *The Last of the Lowries* and was about Robeson County's Henry Berry Lowrie, a type of Robin Hood figure. Some remember Lowrie as an early freedom fighter against white supremacy. Still, in his day, during Reconstruction, there was a bounty for his capture placed by Governor William Woods Holden. Lowrie would now be considered a Lumbee Indian, but at the time Green wrote this play, the Lumbee people, despite that they called themselves Lumbee, after the river they lived along, were widely known as Croatan, the tribe of Hatteras Island, where many believe that at least some of the colonists survived by joining the tribe. Green wasn't the first to write about this, and he did not coin the term "The Lost Colony." As early as the mid-nineteenth century, there was more than one published history called *The Lost Colony of Roanoke*. In the 1890s, a UNC graduate named S. B. Weeks, who'd landed a job teaching history at Trinity College in Randolph County before it moved to Durham and changed its name to Duke, argued that the

Croatan were descendants of the Lost Colony. Some 130 years after Professor Weeks posited that common theory, DNA researchers are now attempting to prove it.

In the Depression, as FDR's New Deal swept through the land and people looked for ways to improve American society with massive building efforts—roads, bridges, dams, and tourist attractions like the Blue Ridge Parkway—a group of local and state leaders imagined a way to help the people of Roanoke Island and lobbied to build a theater and park on Roanoke to commemorate the location of the first English settlement in America, and Paul Green would write what he called a "symphonic drama" to be performed there. Some 200 workers with the Civilian Conservation Corps, a steam shovel, and a mule all camped on the island as they built the groundwork for what is now the Waterside Theater, the setting for the outdoor drama *The Lost Colony*. When the play opened in 1937, President Roosevelt was in attendance. He and most of the audience arrived by ferry, as the road from the mainland had not yet been built.

When it was first suggested to Andy that he take part in the production of *The Lost Colony* in the summer of 1946, he said no, as he could make a bit more money working alongside his father at the furniture factory. He'd been helping out since he was a boy, sweeping up the sawdust and selling cold Cokes on a tray to the workers, and he needed to do real work, make real money. But he hated working in the factory, and after hearing about how great it was in Manteo on Roanoke, he took a cut in pay and joined the cast of *The Lost Colony* the following summer. He made the best friends in his life there: Bob Armstrong,

Ainslie Pryor, Gene and Heleyne McLain, and so many others. And when the owner of a bar across the sound, the Nags Head Beach Club, asked him and his friends to put on a weekly sketch show for his patrons, Andy performed comedy for the first time in his life and got laughs.

3.

In late August of 1970, Andy Griffith floated in a seafoam green buoyed lounge recliner on the clear blue water of the Olympic-size swimming pool behind his 7,000-plus-square-foot Toluca Lake home, a pencil in his mouth, like a horse's bit, and a script in his left hand, a drink and a cigarette in his right. The floating recliner was outfitted with a makeshift ashtray and a drink holder.

Bing Crosby, in the 1930s, to make room for his growing family, had built the large, stately white-columned mansion where Andy and his family live. It had a grand staircase, a marble fireplace in the living room, a billiards room, a wet bar, six bedrooms in the main house, and five additional fireplaces.

Andy's wife Barbara rested in the shade of the cabana—which had a kitchen and full bath—with a view of the pool. She drank an iced cocktail and read a novel; the kids, Sam and Dixie, both of them wiry and blond, suntanned from a summer on North Carolina's Roanoke Island, played together at the other end of the pool. Sam had one of those Clacker toys that were all the rage and tried to get it to clack underwater. Dixie entertained the notion that he might succeed and dunked her head to listen for the clacking sound. The two were at the age where they were too big for Andy to toss in the water from his float. When they were smaller, he'd take a break from his reading to accommodate this bit of mischief: they'd swim over and, held steady in his grip, take turns standing on his shoulders and jumping off the floating recliner. Now they didn't bother him when he was reading scripts.

Lucille Ball had scolded Andy once at the studio, while they were on a break from shooting a CBS promo, that he was always brooding and worrying and said that Andy should take up golf or cards, like Jack Benny, Phil Silvers, and the rest of the boys. He tried but didn't like it much, although he'd go through the motions and play a few holes, since he was a member of the Lakeside Golf Club just down the road, on the other side of Bob Hope's place, and also since his friend and manager, Dick Linke, did a lot of his business there and has just been elected club president.

Andy glanced up from his reading and scanned the roof of his house. The pin oak that Bing and his family planted in the front yard was enormous now and towered over the roof. It needed to be trimmed back before a branch poked a hole in the top floor or the oak leaves got under the shingles and rotted. Architecturally, the house's style was a Hollywood take on a southern colonial but from a distance looked a bit too much like an antebellum southern plantation dropped in the middle of North Hollywood, which was not a good look for the North Carolina native. But in the public imagination, the house was associated with Bing Crosby, since it was featured on postcards at the height of Bing's fame and sold to the busloads of tourists who rode by in trolleys to peek at the stars in their homes—just maybe, hopefully, as they checked their mailbox for a mountain of fan letters or stood by the gate waving as the bus passed. Bing and his wife and children and their pets lived there from the late 1930s until 1943, when the home of the crooner of the most popular song on earth, Irving Berlin's "White Christmas," had a dried-out Christmas tree catch fire that killed a family dog, destroyed their valuables, and made the home unlivable until the damaged sections were rebuilt. Knowing his family and servants were safe and unharmed, that day in January 1943, Bing raced home and pushed past the firefighters to rescue his golf shoes in the front hall, as they had $30,000 in gambling money stuffed in the toes. Bing sold the house and decamped to Beverly Hills but still played golf at Lakeside. The American pin oak was a small sapling when the house was newly built in 1937. Andy eyed it with distrust. It was now giant and almost dwarfed the mansion.

Andy was not associated with the Crosby estate in the public imagination, other than in the minds of his neighbors in Toluca Lake, like his neighbor Bob Hope, who popped by sometimes, as their kids were friends, but Andy is forever linked to the dusty old RKO Forty Acres backlot owned by Desilu Productions, used for exteriors for the fictional town of Mayberry. The same backlot was also used for such disparate productions as *Star Trek*, *Gone with the Wind*, *Gomer Pyle*, *Superman*, *Bonanza*, and *King Kong* and was the setting of dozens of gangster movies, westerns, and B-films that filled lazy Saturday afternoons at the movies for countless children for decades. Yet it is most associated with *The Andy Griffith Show*, a TV sitcom invited inside homes across America and elsewhere and into the hearts of millions—so much so that to many, Mayberry seemed a real town and place that existed at one time, in some misty, not-too-distant past. The show was over, and Andy couldn't escape the character he created, and it frustrated him. He chewed the pencil and focused on the script. On the cover page, the script read THIS IS YOUR LIFE.

It was fitting that Andy bought the Crosby home, as in a way he owed his career to Crosby.

4.

Andy was a skinny teenager grown accustomed to the regular torments of the rough boys who lived around his family's neat little three-room ranch house on the wrong side of Mount Airy, on Haymore Street, near Factory Street where his dad worked at one of several factories in town, the Mount Airy Chair Company. Andy was an only child and liked to sing and clown; the kids called him a mama's boy and made him the patsy and once left him hog-tied inside an empty church vestibule, where he'd run to try and escape them. Sometimes Andy was beaten up just for standing in his front yard.

On a cold night in 1941, Andy escaped to the warmth of the dark movie house in downtown Mount Airy and was transported by the legendary Jack Teagarden's magic on the slide trombone in Bing Crosby's film *Birth of the Blues*. For Crosby, the film was a love letter to jazz. Jazz was the first authentic American art form to capture a world audience and had been all the rage for over thirty years by the time Andy purchased a theater ticket in Mount Airy that day, using the money he'd earned from his National Youth Administration–sponsored custodial job sweeping up the school. A more apt title for the film could be "The Birth of Jazz," as jazz was truly born in New Orleans, and that's the historic moment the film is sort of about.

But calling Bing's movie *Birth of the Blues* or birth of anything is a farce. The film is a fantasy that follows the early life and career of a character named Jeff, who is loosely based on Alcide "Yellow" Nunez, the Creole founder of the Original Dixieland Jazz Band, the first all-white jazz band to play outside New Orleans, in 1917, and the first jazz band to make sound recordings before the word "jazz" was a known expression. When the Victor record label released "Livery Stable Blues," it called the music by a suggested dance, "Fox Trot." Later, the band's leader, Nick LaRocca, falsely claimed that white musicians invented the new genre. Nunez quit the band before its 1917 recording, which may be why Crosby modeled his character on Nunez and the character based on LaRocca was a heel throughout the movie.

The film begins with Jeff as a child, hiding from his conservative father and hanging out on the Basin Street docks, playing music with the Black musicians. He's caught and beaten by his father for crossing this color line and dragged home by his ear, then forced to play only proper classical music. The narrative flashes forward, and Jeff is living in rented rooms with a hodgepodge of jazz musicians, his father long dead. Later, they perform their new music in the street to try to raise money to get a musician out of jail and nearly cause a riot. The townspeople are shocked and offended that they are playing the hot music associated only with Black musicians. The bandmates eventually find a club that will let them perform, once they add a woman singer, played by Mary Martin, who teaches the audience how to dance to the new style of music. A gangster owns the club, and the roster of gangsters in the cabarets and supper clubs in New Orleans features heavily in the plot. Incidentally, the Italian Mafia in America first appears in New Orleans in the 1870s, years before it reaches Chicago and New York.

Birth of the Blues is objectively racist, despite the effort of costar Eddie "Rochester" Anderson and, hopefully, despite Crosby's intentions. Crosby championed jazz musicians his entire life, including Louis Armstrong, who changed music more than any other person in history. They were friends beginning in the 1920s, and Bing was fond of saying, "If you don't like Louis Armstrong, you don't know how to love."

Birth of the Blues attempts to address inequity and intolerance, rather than ignores race entirely, and simply co-opts jazz. Jeff's idea is to deliver jazz—this new American art form, sculpted by Black musicians on a bedrock of blues, ragtime, minstrel music, and military marches—to a white audience. Otherwise, the audience wouldn't listen. Or, if the musicians made up a mixed-race band in the era of Jim Crow, they would not be allowed to play the venue. This isn't addressed in the film, but at the dawn of jazz in New Orleans, the bandleader George Vetiala "Papa Jack" Laine, to whom historians trace the lines of influence of many pioneers of jazz (and with whom Alcide "Yellow" Nunez played early in his career), employed light-skinned African American musicians and simply lied to avoid enforcement of segregation laws, claiming the musicians were Spanish or Cuban.

Jack Teagarden was a white musician and, in the movie that the young Andy Griffith saw in Mount Airy, he is in an all-white band playing Black music, which causes polite society to implode. And this is based on fact. Social leaders, both Black and white, were all in a dither about the popularity of jazz, calling it a low form of entertainment that caused people to move their bodies in ways that resulted in destruction to both the status quo and the aspirations of those who longed to climb to its top.

By 1941, when *Birth of the Blues* played in downtown Mount Airy, Teagarden had been the preeminent trombonist of his cohort for well over a decade. His most famous song is the 1928 Spencer Williams hit, "Basin Street Blues." Historically, Basin Street was inside the New Orleans red-light district, near the French Quarter. Louis Armstrong first recorded and popularized the song the year it was written, when Williams was newly home from France, after collaborating with Josephine Baker and Fats Waller. Teagarden's parents were of German origin, but his birth in Texas's Red River Valley, near the Oklahoma border, might have prompted rumors that he was Cherokee; because of his New Orleans style or his long, intimate association with Louis Armstrong, he is also sometimes mistakenly listed as one of the top African American musicians of all time.

In Ken Burns's documentary film *Jazz*, bandleader and jazz historian Wynton Marsalis, discussing the origins of jazz in nineteenth-century minstrelsy, tells the interviewer, "That was the beginning of a long relationship between Blacks and whites, and Black entertainment and white appropriation of it, and this strange dance we've been doing with each other since really the beginning of our relationship in America. It's too close. It's too deep a story, so you have to degrade the relationship, you have to do degrading things so you can live with the tremendous affront to humanity [that] slavery was."

America's centuries-old obsession with race—with slavery, one-drop policies, Jim Crow, and segregation—

while the nation was the arbiter of freedom in other ways created a conflicting whorl that in New Orleans and elsewhere became a cultural engine and what made *Birth of the Blues* compelling for a poor teenage boy from the wrong side of the little hill town of Mount Airy, North Carolina. Race and class is tightly wound and intertwined around every cultural artifact of America, including Andy Griffith.

Bing Crosby's character in *Birth of the Blues*, the clarinetist, Jeff, is trying to alter white society, not by addressing race and class inequities directly but by getting white people to open their ears to something new and beautiful, loosen up, and smile and laugh and maybe dance. Young Andy sat in the theater, wide-eyed, as Teagarden played trombone and sang the words to "Basin Street Blues":

The band is there to meet us
Old friends to greet us
That's where the light and the dark folks meet
A heaven on earth, they call it Basin Street.

And in that moment, in the dark and smoky Earle Theater on Main Street in Mount Airy, in the shade of the great Blue Ridge, fourteen-year-old Andy Griffith decided his future—a plan for the way forward, to be somebody—and that was to be a bandleader for a swing band.

Andy already had the job sweeping up the school, thanks to Roosevelt's New Deal. On the National Youth Administration application he had lied about his age, as the cutoff was fifteen. It took him about seven months, saving most of his six-dollars-a-month paychecks, and he had enough money for a reconditioned trombone he'd circled in the dog-eared copy of the Spiegel catalog he'd been looking through every night before he said his prayers. Andy's bedroom was unheated. The room had been a back porch, and his father had hammered up walls and enclosed it a few years before. On this cold night, Andy stood by the lit stove in the kitchen, the catalog in hand, and got as hot as he could stand, then ran and dove on his bed, clambering under the stack of patchwork quilts.

5.

Floating in the pool, Andy squinted in the California sun and read through the script. He grabbed at his mouth for the pencil and scribbled the word "No" in the margin, crossing out a word, slashing at it as if he was angry at the sentence for existing. The scriptwriter had given the announcer, Ralph Edwards, a line making fun of Andy's southern accent. "Dumbass." Andy chewed on the word and popped the pencil back in his mouth.

Andy's manager, Dick Linke, had vetted the script for *This Is Your Life* beforehand. For the audience and guest, it all was supposed to be a surprise. It was not. There was too much at stake. There was planning, and travel, and no one could afford surprises. Dick had dropped the script at the house via his Cadillac limo.

Andy grimaced as he read the script. It didn't seem like there was much point to do the show anymore. He didn't want to do it to begin with. When Dick had arranged it, it was to promote his comeback series, *Headmaster*, which had been canceled midseason and replaced with *The New Andy Griffith Show*. That show struggled with ratings as well, and direction; it had almost as much of a tepid critical response as *Headmaster* and was certain to be canceled too. This is your life, indeed. He wasn't hurt by the failure so much as irritated by it. Dick had negotiated the largest contract in history when Andy came back to TV three years after walking away from *The Andy Griffith Show*. With no script or even a format, other than the show would be thirty minutes long, air once a week, and star

Andy Griffith, CBS shook hands on the deal and agreed to upwards of $4 million a year for five years—$20 million—the equivalent of more than $150 million in 2023.

In 1958, Andy had studied his lines in the luxury section of a jet airplane on his way back home to New York to play the lead in an episode of *Playhouse 90*. The performance was a TV adaptation of Elliott Nugent and James Thurber's play, *The Male Animal*, a dramatic comedy that had been made into a film in 1942 starring Henry Fonda as a college professor attacked publicly and threatened with termination after it gets out that he intends to include a scandalous text—a letter Bartolomeo Vanzetti wrote from the Massachusetts death house before his execution—in one of his writing classes. Andy had turned to Dick Linke, seated across the aisle, and asked, "Do you think I should lose my southern accent?" Linke had laughed and answered, "Sure, if you want to try another line of work!" Andy felt as if he owed Dick Linke something, and so he had listened. They were business partners. One of the first investments they made together was a music store in downtown White Plains, near where Dick was living then. Andy and Barbara were in the next town, closer to the water, in Rye, New York. The store sold instruments—winds, strings, horns, percussion—and sheet music and records. Dick's younger brother Bobby had played the horn and the drums; he probably could play anything. And Dick managed musicians, like Tommy Leonetti. But Dick had built a career out of managing Andy Griffith. He had other performers under his umbrella, but Andy was the center. Andy listened to Dick's advice, but he wanted to try the part in *The Male Animal*, Professor Tommy Turner, without much of a southern accent. The character is a literature professor. He would turn the accent way down.

The day after *Playhouse 90* aired, the notices in the trades were horrible. Every one. One reviewer said Andy Griffith should stick to hayseed roles and called him "prissy."

6.

Andy wondered sometimes why Dick had put all his eggs in Andy's basket. When they met, Dick had a good job at Capitol Records. But in those days, the mob controlled the jukeboxes and the nightclubs and the radio DJs routinely took payola. For music publicity, an advance man for a record label would typically show up at a radio station in a rented car with a bottle of whiskey in each hand and a few sex workers, take the DJs out for a good time, and then leave them with a handful of records for the artist the advance man represented, and maybe a handful of cash. Then on to the next town. Wash, rinse, repeat. Maybe Dick was tired and needed a change. But it was trading up. More responsibility, more money, more danger. Before he let Tommy Leonetti go, Dick's arm got busted up somehow.

7.

By Andy Griffith's senior year at the University of North Carolina in 1949, he was a big man on campus. Not the biggest by far—that was reserved for football star Charlie "Choo Choo" Justice, an undersized tailback from the mountain town of Asheville, North Carolina—but Andy was still known and liked among UNC's roughly 6,000 students. Peers and instructors made note of Andy's talent, hard work, and friendly demeanor, although maybe he was a bit nervous and serious. But he hustled, earning extra money at several jobs, not unusual for a working-class kid. Highlighting his vocal talent, he sang at area churches and was paid a few dollars under the table for the effort, thanks to a UNC professor. When a swanky new college bar and restaurant off Franklin Street opened the autumn of his senior year, Andy scored a nightly gig there. He played guitar and sang, roaming between the booths and tables at the cavernous new hangout owned by a Swiss couple, the Danzigers. It was shadowy and low-ceilinged, with dark wood and a giant old wooden door that looked as if it was 400 years old. The bar was in Amber Alley and was called the Ram's Head Rathskeller.

Andy had starred in several school plays, and when the Danzigers promoted their new restaurant to the press, they were sure to mention that Andy Griffith, the lead in the previous year's Gilbert and Sullivan production and Sir Walter Raleigh in the summer production on Roanoke of *The Lost Colony*, would be there most every night to entertain. Another production in which Andy was cast as the lead was a one-act play written by his friend Bob Armstrong. It was produced and performed by the Carolina Playmakers, and the piece of original writing landed Armstrong a graduate fellowship at UNC. The play was called *Egypt Land* and was inspired by the life of Huddie Ledbetter, known professionally as Lead Belly. After touring and singing for two decades around Louisiana and Texas and finding himself in and out of jail for various charges in the Jim Crow South, Ledbetter, beginning in the 1930s and working with folklorists John and Alan Lomax, gathered folk songs across the South and recorded and performed them for an international audience, spurring the first wave of the folk revival in American music. In 1950, the Weavers had a number one hit with Lead Belly's "Goodnight, Irene." Sometimes Andy sang "In the Pines" and other Lead Belly songs in his act.

The central characters, including the lead in Armstrong's play, were Black, but at that historic moment UNC was segregated. Bob, an Alabama steelworker and the first person in his family to go to college, told his friend Andy that Andy was the only person there who could play the lead. The poor southern white was a stand-in for Black Americans in a segregated entertainment field. It was as if America could not address racial disparity directly. As Wynton Marsalis put it, "It's too close. It's too deep a story." Only a few years later Andy Griffith arrived on the American entertainment scene along with other white southern performers such as Elvis and Jerry Lee Lewis.

At UNC in 1949, in addition to two summers as Sir Walter Raleigh in *The Lost Colony*, Andy was the president of the Glee Club, had been featured in vocal recitals at Hill Hall, and was a member of the Phi Mu Alpha music fraternity. He had leadership qualities and was ambitious. He was elected president of Battle dorm a few years after he had set his pajamas, blankets, and room 9 on fire, falling asleep with a lit cigarette—his peers forgave him. Andy was recruited to help organize the headlining event for Sadie Hawkins Day and directed a "floorshow of outstanding hillbilly talent," where the price of admission was an Appalachian costume. Some wore overalls and walked around barefoot. Andy heeded the reaction that received from his classmates. He'd sometimes assume this persona around his first wife's parents, going shirtless and barefoot, gleefully understanding it aggravated their class prejudice and ideas about propriety.

Andy played sousaphone in the Tar Heel marching band and was in formation at all the football games. Charlie "Choo Choo" Justice twice led the team to the Sugar Bowl in New Orleans. Andy had never seen so many people in his life. Those games broke attendance records. Charlie Justice was twice nominated for a Heisman trophy, was a two-time first-team All-American, and was on the cover of *Life* magazine Andy's senior year. One can't overstate the phenomenon of Charlie "Choo Choo" Justice. (The only UNC athlete to surpass Justice in fame was Michael Jordan decades later.) Before the Buncombe County native landed in Chapel Hill, fresh from the navy and married, the UNC football program had not been all that competitive; Justice put the team in the national spotlight. An eight-and-a-half-foot-tall bronze statue of Justice stands outside the entrance of the Kenan Football Center on UNC–Chapel Hill's lush campus, wearing his number 22 and carrying his helmet. Justice was offered a football scholarship but instead used the GI Bill to pay for college and asked UNC if his scholarship could be given to his wife to join Chapel Hill's freshman class, and the university agreed.

Andy witnessed firsthand the passion fans had for football and the fame swirling around Charlie Justice. He took in the fanaticism and the almost religious fervor—and also experienced bullying by drunken fans, who sometimes dumped beer into his giant horn.

A few years after college, Andy and Barbara borrowed money from his father's bosses at the furniture mill, printed a brochure, quit their teaching jobs, and lit out on the road to entertain Rotarians, Associations of Volunteer Firefighters, and insurance executives—any club or civic group that would pay for the privilege. Their first job was in 1952 at the Asheboro Rotary Club. William A. "Red" Underwood Jr. is credited with hiring the pair and giving them their first gig. The Griffiths were paid seventy-five dollars to entertain the good Rotarians of Asheboro, North Carolina.

Not too long after that first performance, Andy wrote "What It Was, Was Football," the comedy monologue that would thrust him onto the national stage. Barbara had double-booked them at a convention in Raleigh, and Andy wrote the football bit on the way to the show. Playing his horn at all those games—even when fans had thrown beer at him—paid off.

At the apogee of Charlie Justice's fame at UNC, an alum named Orville Campbell cowrote a swinging jazz song about Justice called "All the Way Choo Choo." Andy had seen Campbell stalking around campus, well dressed and with a neat part in his hair. And in 1950, walking in the shade of the giant poplars on campus, one could hear the tune blaring out of a dormitory window or from an AM car radio as a load of kids cruised with open windows down Franklin Street. Johnny Long and his Orchestra recorded the song in 1949, with Janet Brace and the Glee Club providing vocals. Benny Goodman and His Orchestra had also performed the music live in 1949, as Campbell attempted to convince Goodman's label, Capitol Records, to include "All the Way Choo Choo" on Goodman's next album. Capitol declined, as it considered the song too regional. However, it put Orville Campbell on Capitol's radar. The song also made Campbell enough money to launch another company, Colonial Records, and the company he had already established, Colonial Publishing. With an influx of cash, Campbell went about looking for more talent to record.

For three days in early April 1953, the third annual Southern Short Course in Photography was held on UNC's campus, chaired by Hugh Morton, which for a nominal fee provided participants "a unique opportunity to obtain expert instruction in the latest photographic processes and techniques." Barbara and Andy were the entertainment portion of the event at a luncheon at the Carolina Inn. Morton paid the couple twenty-five dollars. Since the venue was in town and the Griffiths didn't have to travel, they took the job at a low rate. Andy's monologues got big laughs from the assembled news photographers, photo editors, and enthusiasts. Orville Campbell was in attendance, there to improve his publishing operation with the latest news in photo technology and maybe meet a few newspaper veterans. To his good fortune, he stumbled across a way forward with Colonial Records as well. Campbell approached Andy after the show, asking if he'd like to make a recording.

A few months later, to a crowd of insurance industry professionals assembled at a Jefferson Standard Insurance Company dinner held at the Jefferson Standard Country Club just northwest of Greensboro, North Carolina, Andy performed "What It Was, Was Football," among other monologues, with the expert recording assistance of a Greensboro teenager named Milton Alderfer.

Over the next months, Andy visited Milton at the little studio he rented over Moore Music on West Market Street in Greensboro, just across the street from leafy Greensboro College and in sight of the city's only skyscraper, the Jefferson Standard building at the center of town. When it opened in 1923, it was the tallest building between Atlanta and DC. Will Rogers visited Greensboro and said the locals "were as proud of the one building on its skyline as parents are of a baby's first tooth!" A professor of mine at the University of North Carolina–Greensboro, Jim Clark, claimed when the building was first lit, people outside of town saw it on the horizon and thought the world was ending.

Above the music store, Andy and Milton Alderfer edited the master recording, tweaking the laughter and audience response until Andy had it exactly as he wanted. Moore Music still exists in Greensboro. I bought a Yamaha acoustic guitar for my girlfriend there in 1994. But the old mansion with giant Corinthian columns and a rounded porch, where the Moore family set up shop and where Andy climbed the steps to the office upstairs, is no more. Alderfer sent the reel to Orville Campbell, and the waxed pressing came out November 14, 1953. Three pressings sold out in a month, and by December 7, Capitol Records bought the master for $10,000, split 50-50 between Andy and Orville.

The site where the country club existed in Greensboro is now owned by the city and is home to the Kathleen Clay Edwards Family Branch Library, located in Price Park. The park is almost 100 acres and has a butterfly meadow, walking trails, and pond but no sign that this was the spot where Andy Griffith recorded the hit that launched his career—although if one stood in the cul-de-sacs in the bordering neighborhoods on an early evening in the warm weather, you might hear the theme music of *The Andy Griffith Show*.

In 1973, many years after UNC and a brief but successful career in the NFL, and as Andy Griffith was beamed into America's homes daily and was one of the highest paid TV actors in history, Charlie Justice lived in a modest home in Greensboro, not far from where Andy recorded "What It Was, Was Football." Charlie Justice was working in the insurance industry in Greensboro, not for Jefferson Standard but under his own shingle, and in a feature for *Sports Illustrated*, ruminating on his legacy, Justice told the reporter, "I suppose I could have been a lot of things. A musician, maybe, or even an artist, but what I was was a football player, and that's all I ever wanted to be." Back in the 1950s, Orville Campbell promised Justice some of the royalties from "All the Way Choo Choo," but Justice never saw a dime.

8.

My mom's dad, Wallace Simmons, was Andy Griffith's third cousin, although I doubt they knew each other any more than in passing, nodding at the counter of the Weiner-Burger on Rockford Street, a little restaurant ran by Andy's cousin Evan Moore. Andy worked for a while at the Weiner-Burger as a teenager and developed his love of hot dogs. Wallace and my grandmother Sallie Dalton Simmons would walk to Rockford Street in downtown Mount Airy and take their kids for a burger and a Coke, and maybe some Gibson's ice cream every now and again, if they had any spare coins. Sometimes they met there after Sallie finished her shift at the giant mill in the middle of town, on Willow Street, the Mount Airy Knitting Company. Sallie and all of Wallace's sisters worked there, standing on the assembly line, all day every day, making the same stitches on clothing for infants. Andy knew he was a Simmons, but there were so many Simmonses around Surry County it was impossible to keep track.

What I know of Wallace is mostly negative: he was a chain-smoking, hardworking weekend drunk, a combat veteran who called in sick to his job at the granite quarry if it was raining. He died at the age of fifty-four of white lung, or silicosis, a long-term disease caused by inhaling silica dust from the quarry. It could have been exacerbated by something he picked up in the Philippines, where he spent a good portion of World War II. Lots of men brought home bacterial infections in their lungs from tropical climates. Whatever the case, he was healthy enough to reenlist in the army during the Korean War. I recall hearing that Wallace had served in two branches of the armed services and remarking to my grandmother Sallie that he must have loved his country, and she took a drag off her Kool Mild 100 and said in her soft, sad way from the spot where she always stood at the far corner of the kitchen counter, "Well, the money was good. Better than working in that quarry in Mount Airy."

My mother had a wallet-size photo of her father as a young man, wearing a leather jacket, his hair greased back, looking a little like Gary Cooper, the actor who would break the young Patricia Neal's heart after filming *Bright Leaf* (1950), causing what Neal called her first nervous breakdown. Of her father, Mom said, "My girlfriends in high school thought he was handsome. And that made me proud of him. But he was weak. He and Mama would send me and my sister to the landlord or to the electric company to tell them we couldn't pay our bill, to the grocery store and ask for credit." Mom remembered how he would drink too much and be cross and violent and then hold them and blubber and apologize. It disgusted her and made her ashamed. When I was in college, my roommate and I let our landline phone get disconnected because neither of us ever seemed to have at the exact same moment the seventeen bucks we each needed to pay it. Mom called me out in my driveway and said I was soft and told me I reminded her of her father.

Wallace died when I was a toddler—the only memory I have of him is a tall shadow standing in the doorway with a thick head of shining, jet-black pomaded hair—he looked like he could be Andy Griffith's cousin.

Andy represented a version of a man in my family who could transcend his mill worker status and rise above the trappings of abuse and alcohol, although if we asked Andy, I'm not sure he'd agree. He eventually quit abusing alcohol, not long after my grandfather Wallace died in 1971. Wallace dropped dead in the flowerbed in his front yard of their rented home. He had been complaining that morning of not feeling well, and Mom told him to quit bellyaching and work in the yard, maybe the fresh air would do him some good.

After the open-air funeral arranged by Mount Airy's Moody Funeral Home at Skyline Memory Garden cemetery, my mother stopped eating. Like Patricia Neal, Mom called this her first nervous breakdown. Dad had her hospitalized. In 1971, I was three. I remember one single thing about the funeral. Moody's had laid down Astroturf for the ceremony, covering the fresh dirt and protecting the grass of the graveyard. The Astroturf fascinated me, so I knelt down to rub my fingers across its texture, and Mom bent over, pinched me hard as hell, and hissed, "Stop." That would be about the last time I'd see any of Wallace's family, still working in the Mount Airy clothing mill, although it had changed its name to Spencer's Infant's and Children's Wear. It's a shame our evolution makes those jarring, frightened memories the ones we're left with. That's how we survive. We wouldn't be here without it, likely. Dinosaurs would have eaten all our ancestors. Spencer's is empty now, the baby blue sprawling factory at the center of Mount Airy, but is to be developed into apartments and shops.

9.

In 2015, I lived in Beacon, New York, and drove each week to Cambridge, Massachusetts, to be with my children. For most of that year, I rented a hotel suite somewhere near Cambridge and stayed for the weekend—which ate up most of my sad income—as they had weekend activities that could not be missed.

With normal traffic and breaking the speed limit, the drive is two and a half hours one way, but driving back to New York after dropping the kids off, I was in no hurry, as I had nothing to come home to, and would drive the back roads and state highways to avoid the Mass Pike, often by necessity, as I'd have no money left to pay tolls. Since I left Manhattan, my car was the only place I felt comfortable. As long as I was inside the cab of that ancient light-green Subaru Outback, my life had not irrevocably changed.

On one of those Sunday evenings, after dropping the kids off at their mother's townhouse near Harvard, I wound my way west, ambling and turning, not caring which route I took, which little two-lane colonial cow path, past the bedroom communities and villages that surround Boston. My car had a compass underneath the rearview mirror, and I tried to keep it pointing west by southwest. Driving through the country was soothing. At times I found the staid colonial architecture boring and rigid but every so often was struck by a postcard scene, a Currier and Ives print, a snowy field and a farmhouse in the distance, the sunlight bending through a forest, a brook meandering through the trees interrupted by a beaver dam and then oozing out into a low swamp. And as a child of NASCAR, I enjoyed driving on the winding roads, roads that had likely been trod on by paw and hoof and human foot for thousands of years. Subaru's boxer engines are mounted low, so even a boring old dad wagon like a 2001 Outback handles and banks curves well.

After I'd hug my kids goodbye and carry their bags to their mother's porch and hop back in the Outback, at first, in the earliest days, with the windows rolled up, I'd be screaming at the top of my lungs by the first stoplight at the end of the block. As time passed, weeks, months, as it does, maybe an hour after I dropped my kids off, on the Pike, I'd scream. I'd wail if traffic moved fast enough for me to go unnoticed, rocking back and forth, spewing a vicious spray of curses and invectives. Then, months later, the screaming came in shorter bursts after I passed into New York. Then, a year or so later, no matter where I was, I stopped screaming in the car entirely. Back in Massachusetts, for most of 2016, I screamed only in the shower when no one else was home, and then by 2017 I stopped screaming altogether. The only guttural sounds I made were straining to lift something, typically a pallet of thirty-two fifty-pound cases of bananas at my job at the grocery store.

One of those evenings, driving west, somewhere on Route 30, maybe between Wellesley and Natick, passing the darkened manor houses and tall trees along the lonely old post road, the green light from the dash of the Outback glowing, a song came on the radio, the Avett Brothers' "I and Love and You."

I knew the story behind the song. The North Carolina bandmates, who grew up in the countryside outside Concord, North Carolina, near Charlotte, wrote that song after feeling out of their element at their first show in New York City, at Galapagos, when it was still based in Williamsburg, Brooklyn, in an old warehouse near the East River, low-lit with tea candles floating in a few inches of dark water the owners had flooded the concrete floors with at the entrance alongside an elevated walkway. It was a huge, magical space and quite a scene. My soon-to-be-bride and I, together with our good friends, went there the night before we married, and the Galapagos house band played at our wedding. The line has a taste of Thomas Wolfe in it, "Oh, Brooklyn...take me in."

Somewhere around Wellesley, I pulled the car over to the side of the small road and turned on the hazard lights. I started bawling. I didn't have my family. I didn't have a home.

10.

The ambulance driver raced along Highway 64, down the flat sandy stretch in Manteo, heading toward the great ocean. Route 64 is a national highway stretching all the way across North Carolina, from Murphy to Manteo, which gave the state a slogan and line in a song to recruit visitors. The state tourism board's commercial played on local television, all during my youth, along with *The Andy Griffith Show*. The road crosses the Tennessee line in Cherokee County and cuts through the top center of the Old North State from the rolling Piedmont through the massive stretch of low-lying Sand Hills and its peanut farms, sharecropper shacks, and fruit stands—where one can still buy a bag of boiled peanuts for a dollar or two. It passes the stretch of Asheboro, in the dead center of the state, where I mostly grew up, in a suburban neighborhood build on pastureland in the modern style, in the late 1960s and early 1970s, and given a ludicrous sheriff of Nottingham–style name, Westbury Woods. I'd stand at the edge of my driveway and watch the cars drive past in the autumn, imagining college kids traveling from their homes somewhere toward Charlotte northeast to Chapel Hill or Durham or Raleigh. The highway ends, or begins, depending on your version of the story, in the west near the famed Four Corners in northeastern Arizona and ends and/or begins again in Nags Head, near Whalebone Junction.

11.

It was early morning; we were heading home to Asheboro from visiting my grandmother in Mount Airy. My sister was thirteen years old in the passenger seat; I was nine, in the back, sitting between the seats of the 1971 sky-blue VW station wagon, screaming. My mother was at the wheel, eyes half closed, mouth half open in a weird grimace, saliva dripping out of the side. She was making odd, choky noises in her throat, as if snoring while clearing her nostrils and trying to swallow, all at the same time. She'd taken too many pills, or mixed medications, or something, and was half out of her skull. We were driving the right direction toward the little town we lived in but were on the wrong side of the highway, facing oncoming traffic. Luckily—and I am indeed lucky—there was no oncoming traffic.

12.

All day in kindergarten class at the Fayetteville Street Christian School in Asheboro, North Carolina, Glen had spoken of his new space guns. A matching set. They were gleaming blue and metal gray and shot spinning, colored disks in all the colors of the rainbow that flew for what seemed days. The disks were slightly larger than a quarter and looked something like the plastic widgets designed to hold a 45-rpm record in place on a stereo turntable. I had seen them for sale in the toy aisle at Mann's Drugstore and knew exactly the ones Glen was talking about. I wanted to play with them. I wanted to see them and shoot them and see the disks fly. I wanted to have a blast. Glen asked if I wanted to play at his house after school. We each asked our parents when they arrived at 2:15 p.m. to pick us up. Glen's mother said it was OK. My dad told me we were going to my grandmother's house in Winston-Salem— where my mom's mother lived—and that I should come with him, as she was expecting us. Glen's face grew dark, and Glen's mother touched my dad's forearm and said, "Bob, doesn't Evan get car sick? That's a long drive each way to Mrs. Simmons's house. You can pick him up after. We'll take care of him." My dad agreed and said we could stop in on my grandmother driving back from Mount Airy on Sunday, after visiting his mother, my other grand-mother. I ran and jumped in Glen's family wagon, and my dad walked back to his tan VW Beetle and was off to his mother-in-law's to deliver some leftover Halloween pumpkins so she could make pie.

At Glen's, we played for hours. We snacked, we watched TV, and we played with other toys, but most of all we warred with each other with those blue space guns, the spinning disks wheeling magically down the long hall of the suburban split-level, the colors bright against the dark-stained, knotty pine wood-paneled walls. They seemed to suspend in air, fly forever, bounce off walls and ceiling, and keep on.

My sister Logan had arrived after school with Glen's older sister Karen. They were in Karen's room playing with the door closed. We were told to keep out. To stay in the hall. The phone rang. I heard low voices. Later it rang again. I heard a succession of doors close between where Glen and I were playing and the rest of the house. It was getting dark now. Headlights bounced off the sheer curtains on the front picture windows of the darkened formal living room. No one played in there, as it was intended for guests and was where the good furniture was kept. The phone rang yet again. After a time, Glen's mother cracked open the door and said our mother was running late, she'd be there to pick Logan and me up soon, and when she arrived we were to go out to the car. Then the door shut. I heard another door click shut. The phone rang yet again. More headlights. The spinning yellow disk was beautiful. And now an orange one. A light blue one. The color of a robin's egg. Glen and I shot a round each from either end of the long hallway. I watched them fly above my head, and each one made time stop. A miracle. I loved it. It made me so happy. So much joy. And I never saw my dad again.

Just as Glen's mom had said, our mother arrived in her Carolina blue VW Wagon and was sitting behind the driver's seat, in the driveway, the headlights off. As soon as we climbed in the car, my sister in the front and me in the back, my mom, looking straight ahead, stone-faced and pale, her voice low, said, "Your dad is dead. There was an accident."

I recall my sister and me bawling, and our mother starting the car, and her telling us there were going to be a lot of people at the house and not to be afraid and that if we wanted to be alone we should find a room and lock the door, and when we got home it seemed the whole world was inside our house. Cars were parked along the road and in the yard. Inside it seemed everyone had a casserole dish in hand.

This is my core grief. This one domino set into motion many grievous things to come. One by one, knocked them down. There are tragedies in every life, and there were more to come in mine that had little to nothing to do with that first and greatest pain. Yet it's the one I come back to again and again. This overarching grief. This moment. When a terrible early and violent death happened. My young dad, who'd served in the U.S. Army in Occupied Germany and brought home a not uncommon affection for the ridiculous VW Beetle, was hit head-on by an overly medicated elderly lady in a giant green American-made Buick who crossed the double line into his lane on Old Thomasville Road, and Dad was crushed by the steering column plunging the steering wheel into his broad chest, as there is no engine in the front of those stupid Nazi cars. He'd not had the design flaw replaced with a collapsible steering column, which VW would have paid for, as this way of dying had happened enough that the company had designed a safer steering column the year before and replaced them for free, to avoid paying out millions more dollars in wrongful death suits.

So this is my grief. The story I tell over and over. You have your grief. I have mine. If we are in the same family, we may share our grief. If we're in the same community, we may grieve together when something tragic happens, and something tragic is always happening. Nations grieve. War and natural disaster. The world grieves. War and famine. Disease and random accident. Life is a constant state of grief. It's not like traveling from one town to another or sitting in a bright room and suddenly the lights go out. It's the air we breathe. It's the currents of electricity powering everything. Just as change is a constant. It's not something that happens; it's something that is always happening. Graveyards are at the centers of towns. The parlor in a home is called a parlor because that's where people came to view the body and say goodbye. In recent decades the parlor was moved outside the home and made into a business called funeral parlors. It's as if restaurants were called Sandwich Kitchens. Funerals were removed from the home, and parlors were rebranded as living rooms. The makers of *The Andy Griffith Show* knew this, that the world is full of grief. They had fought in World War II and seen bodies torn apart; their parents had escaped pogroms or had fought in the First World War and come home shell-shocked. Some of their first memories were of watching their homes set on fire by Cossacks. They were children of immigrants and had lived through the Depression. When *The Andy Griffith Show* aired in the 1960s, the civil rights movement and its torturous abuses and killings, combined with the growing chaos of Vietnam, the jet age, political assassinations—all the anxieties and grief of the modern age—were at play. But Monday nights on CBS, *The Andy Griffith Show* provided a meditative balm.

After the pandemic's arrival in 2020, with its onslaught of fear and anxiety, illness, and death and with hospitals and morgues past the breaking point, viewership of *The Andy Griffith Show* and other beloved reruns rose. In anxious times people turn to the familiar, to nostalgia, for comfort. Psychologists refer to the huge amounts of stress taxing our brain's ability to form new memories as "cognitive load"—so we replay older memories. And the way subjects' brains light up under imaging devices, like an MRI, indicates they watch reruns with no deficit of joy. The scan is the same, as if they are watching the show again for the first time. Most reported more pleasure seeing a show they'd already seen before.

13.

Walking along the broken sidewalk, the noise of trucks and cars going about their business from every angle, one might find this street unremarkable for this part of the Bronx, less interesting. It's mostly treeless, with neat, low apartment buildings on one side and, on the other, a giant New York City Sanitation facility, built to house the city's army of street sweepers. Like many modern NYC government structures, it has the air of a fortress, made of red brick, but it is also a kind of industrial building built in the 1970s and 1980s that one might see anywhere—a biology building on a college campus in Iowa, or a courthouse in a North Carolina suburb. It reminds me of One Police Plaza downtown, which for years I walked past every day on my way to work and wondered why they built it on an elevation facing down to the east, where the poor people lived. It seemed intentional. Then during the Occupy Wall Street months, I saw firsthand why. The troopers in their fetish-y black trench coats and assault weapons lined the building, facing down to Water Street. Traditionally, any city's poor lived by the water, especially in New York, because that was where its docks and factories and tanneries stood, where animals were rendered, where the sewers led to the water, where the horse manure was dumped. The wealthy people lived inland to avoid the stench—and also to avoid the poor who did all the work. It was only in recent decades that developers eyed all that real estate and began pressuring for change. Mike Bloomberg made a more significant contribution to income inequality than any NYC mayor in history, changing the laws so luxury high-rises could be built along the water.

Here in the Bronx, on East 175th Street, the city didn't stop at the building's façade. The red bricks continue, extending out from the sanitation building, oozing out onto the sidewalk, which at one time may have been an interesting visual but now is loose and broken, and giant sections of the brick sidewalk are cracked and gone— maybe disposed of, or reused, or taken by someone in need of a decent brick. The architects designed planters the length of the front for landscaping that are mostly cracked and empty, except for a few small, long-suffering trees. The Cross-Bronx Expressway is just on the other side of the giant structure, and its steady engine thrums at all hours. If you've driven on I-95 heading north out of Manhattan, you have passed here likely not thinking much about it, except to hope that traffic keeps moving so you can get upstate for the weekend to go apple picking or see the autumn leaves in their glory. Crotona Park is only a few blocks south, with its many ball fields, hand-ball courts, and a lake, but here, this street is mixed-use for habitat and industry, and in 1956 it is where Gold Medal Studios stood. Newly restored and renamed by Herbert Poll, the studio had been called by the far more famous name of Biograph Studios when the facility was built in 1912. Biograph was the largest film studio on the East Coast and, on sixty-one sets, was where Andy Griffith, Patricia Neal, Walter Matthau, Lee Remick, Anthony Franciosa, Elia Kazan, Budd Schulberg, and the rest filmed most of the interiors of *A Face in the Crowd*. The exterior shooting began in August of 1956 in Arkansas,

Memphis, and Missouri. On day one of principal photography, Andy Griffith saw a film camera for the first time.

If you are in New York City and see one of those small, nimble trucks with the giant wet rolling brushes doing the constant and impossible work of attempting to keep the city streets clean and free of all manner of refuse, sandwich wrappers, cigarette butts, and shit, know that it may rest at night in the location of a cultural palace.

14.

In 2013, about fifteen years into my marriage in New York City to a writer I met in graduate school, which included years as a stay-at-home dad, I was three years into a new full-time office career as an editor and finally began seriously pursuing writing. I made room for myself to work: space at home, space in my head and in the running conversation about the domestic world. I began speaking aloud my ideas and hopes. I began pitching ideas to magazine editors. I sold a pitch for a long essay to an upstart online literary review based in Los Angeles. I worked for months on the essay. I began it after the actor Andy Griffith died. It was about Andy Griffith. But it was also about our ideas about fathers, our desire and nostalgia for things that didn't exist, our ability to superimpose our beliefs over unrelated subjects. And it was also about me. It was about 8,000 words. I was paid $100 for it.

15.

In the sleepy, sylvan community of Taylor, Georgia, a child was shackled to a tree. The small girl—we don't know her name, as she was under eighteen and protected by the laws of Georgia—was adopted by a couple named Diana and Samuel Franklin, who locked her in an outhouse as punishment and outfitted the child with a dog's shock collar that the Franklins operated by remote control. The girl cried all night and all day, and no one came. This went on and on. The Franklins beat the naked child with a belt buckle, tied her to a tree, locked her in a chicken coop, and meticulously detailed disciplinary measures in a journal. The Franklins were zealous in their intention to cure the girl of her humanity.

An anonymous tip sent social workers to the property, followed by the sheriff, where they found the girl padlocked in a garage. She'd not been allowed to attend school or have friends or wear proper clothes or live in any way a normal life. All was punishment for the sin of living, the crime of being a person in the world. The parents were tried separately. At Diana Franklin's trial, defending her actions before she was sentenced to 129 years in prison for forty-seven counts of abuse and neglect, she admonished the sheriff for not being more like Andy Griffith. The judge scolded Franklin, saying she would get better treatment in jail than she gave her daughter. A reporter covering the case wrote, "This child wasn't locked in a chicken coop and beaten naked in Mayberry."

16.

I started a book proposal. An agent was interested in seeing it. Then my wife, a successful writer by that time, very suddenly (to me) left me for a man she'd dated in college, twenty years before.

Not long after this shattering event, sitting in my office in lower Manhattan I received a phone call from a member of a literary society in North Carolina. The person had read my essay on Andy Griffith and invited me to come speak at the group's annual conference in the state capital of Raleigh. I said sure and continued my daily process of getting home from work and, after entering my empty apartment, stumbling through the rooms and wailing like a gutshot wolf, drinking beer until I fell asleep, and getting up the next day and doing it all over again.

A few months later I boarded a train in Manhattan bound for North Carolina. I was wearing what was my then standard attire for appearing in the world, an outfit appropriate for a struggling adjunct professor—an eighteen-year-old brown-checkered Burlington Coat Factory wool sport coat and nineteen-dollar black Wrangler jeans from Target. I had packed my one suit bought on sale for the last wedding I'd attended five years earlier, before all my friends began their steady trudge through divorce, and in my backpack I carried my clunky old computer, my notes on Andy Griffith, and a yellow legal pad on which I'd numbered the pages 1 through 23 to correspond with twenty-three digital files I'd gathered in the days before.

Since twenty-three was Michael Jordan's number, I felt it was a lucky number for a visit to North Carolina.

Before I'd boarded the train I'd created a slideshow with twenty-three slides. I'd rehearsed a few times and intended to outline and further rehearse my talking points for each slide during the twelve-hour train ride from New York City to Durham. It would be a casual discussion on a topic I thought I knew a lot about: my thoughts about Andy Griffith and his role in our culture.

17.

In 2004, in Hollywood, four kids with fishing poles sat onstage, pretending to fish to *The Andy Griffith Show* theme music, played by a full orchestra inside a giant Los Angeles pavilion, where round dinner tables draped in white linens were laden with flowers and wine glasses and small plates of food. Andy Griffith and the composer Earle Hagen stood in tuxedos, whistling behind them and snapping along to the music. Moments before, gold lamé–clad dancers had wheeled onstage the surviving cast of *The Beverly Hillbillies*, who stood in a box made to suggest a tiny pickup truck and sang a portion of their show's theme song. And before that, the spectacle had begun with a mezzo-soprano and a basso profundo singing a song written for the evening to the familiar bouncing theme of *Gilligan's Island*.

Just before the lights dimmed and the music changed and the focus shifted from the side stage where Andy Griffith and Earle Hagen stood, the four children with fishing poles dressed like Opie, one with red hair, got up to leave the stage. The elderly Earle Hagen and Andy Griffith opened their arms and leaned down to hug the kids as they scrambled past, tousling their hair, patting their backs in a fatherly way. One boy shot past Hagen, but Andy, following the cue discussed in rehearsal, bent his legs, widened his arms, and wrapped two kids in a quick hug to conclude the segment. Perhaps that's why the show's producer selected four Opies, rather than one—to make sure at least one got a hug. Andy got two of them.

18.

Eight dollars garners admission to the Andy Griffith Museum in Mount Airy, North Carolina. The unadorned brick building opened in 2009 on a bluff across from the Andy Griffith Playhouse, with a ribbon cutting held on the twentieth anniversary of Mayberry Days, the town's annual celebration of *The Andy Griffith Show*. Mount Airy, located in North Carolina's northwestern Piedmont, near the Virginia line, is where Andy grew up poor and ambitious, and its people claim inspiration for the fictional town at his eponymous show's center. Andy steadfastly refuted this common belief and attended Mayberry Days only once, five years earlier in 2004, in his second official Mount Airy public appearance since 1957, back when the town held an "Andy Griffith Appreciation Day" (the same year my mother, the teenage Betty Jean Simmons, rode with other contestants of the Miss Mount Airy Beauty Pageant in a convertible driven by my dad, Bobby Lee Smith). Like Andy, my parents at birth had each been given a nickname as their legal name and, despite education and accomplishment, shared a nagging embarrassment at the class implications—Andy instead of Andrew, Bobby rather than Robert, Betty instead of Elizabeth. My parents used initials in lieu of full names in the thin phonebook of the North Carolina town we settled in. Andy corrected people who made the mistake—although not the producers of the television show *Biography*, who in their 1997 gloss of Andy Griffith's life and career got it wrong, naming him Andrew Samuel Griffith.

His most famous character was named Andrew Jackson Taylor. The man himself was Andy.

In 2004, a bronze statue was dedicated in Mount Airy, picturing a scene from *The Andy Griffith Show*'s opening: Sheriff Andy Taylor holding hands with his son, Opie, fishing poles resting on shoulders. (The statues are only slightly larger than life—visitors pose with arms around them, pat their backs, place hands on heads.) The ceremony took place outside the Andy Griffith Playhouse, and the then seventy-eight-year-old actor smiled determinedly, gave an informative and lighthearted speech touching on the history of the show, emphasizing the diverse backgrounds of its makers, and politely avoided renouncing the town's claims by punctuating the speech with references to Mount Airy as "where the show was born," meaning where *he* was born.

The little town of Mount Airy, situated in the shadow of the Blue Ridge Mountains, counts tourism its second largest industry (behind agriculture), with the force of visitors climbing steadily in the years since Mayberry Days launched and arriving in record numbers in the months after Andy Griffith was buried in the sandy loam outside his sixty-acre home in Manteo, North Carolina, over 300 miles away from his birthplace, in July 2012. Travelers to Mount Airy are welcome to stay in the humble mill-hand ranch house where Andy lived as a child— it's now a bed-and-breakfast. There are numerous other businesses with either a connection to the show or fashioned as tribute, including the original Snappy Lunch, Floyd's Barbershop, the Bluebird Diner, a faithfully replicated Mayberry courthouse interior—with dual jail cells and a candlestick phone on which fans pretend to speak with Sarah, Mayberry's lone operator—and Wally's Service Station, where a mini-fleet of Ford Galaxie 500s painted to look like a Mayberry squad car provide round-the-clock tours.

The first curator of the Andy Griffith Museum was Emmett Forrest, a lifelong friend raised in the same south-end section of town, near the factories, where Andy was called "white trash" as a child. Elia Kazan used this gnawing hurt to draw a performance out of Griffith during the filming of *A Face in the Crowd.* According to Gilbert Millstein, who profiled Griffith for the *New York Times Magazine* in 1957, Kazan would growl in a low voice "white trash" at Andy just before rolling camera, and as J. W. Williamson put it in his book *Hillbillyland,* "The fury of the outsider would rise in the actor like Lucifer in starlight." Griffith told Millstein he was so troubled by his immersion in the character he played in *A Face in the Crowd*—the everyman entertainer turned megalomaniac Larry "Lonesome" Rhodes—that he and his first wife, Barbara, almost quit show business. Andy said, "It took three months to shoot it, and two months to get over it." Jeff Bridges recounted learning from Andy while shooting *Hearts of the West* that "after working with director Elia Kazan on *A Face in the Crowd* and being taken to the depths into emotional areas that Andy didn't really enjoy, he vowed to not do any projects that took him in that direction."

Instead of quitting the business, he and Barbara left New York City, vacating an Upper East Side apartment for the newly bought home in Manteo. Manteo was where he and Barbara had starred a decade earlier in a "symphonic outdoor drama," *The Lost Colony*, commemorating the history of the first English colonists on Roanoke Island. (*The Lost Colony* is still running.)

Starting around 2007, once a month or more, Betty Lynn—the actress who played Barney's girlfriend, Thelma Lou, in the show's first five seasons—frequented the museum and signed 8 ×10 headshots for ten bucks. At the encouragement of other cast members, Lynn first visited North Carolina to attend Mayberry Days in 2001. She had lived in the same West Hollywood three-bedroom home since 1950 but moved into a Mount Airy retirement community in 2007. After years of speaking to devotees of *The Andy Griffith Show*, Lynn believed a central reason that fans love the show is because they wish Andy was their father—she heard this again and again, especially from men. Sheriff Andy Taylor was a surrogate for fathers who were absent, remote, or brutal.

19.

On the morning of July 3, 2012, after the news arrived that Andy Griffith had died at his home in coastal North Carolina, I thought about sharing my enthusiasm for *The Andy Griffith Show* with my children after discovering its eight seasons streaming on Netflix. I wanted to leave my office and spend the remainder of the day sitting by the river, which I couldn't actually do and keep my job. So there I sat in a mesh office chair instead, sending out some messages on Twitter, reading the flickering remembrances of others, and watching clips.

Social media divides our attention, perhaps, but it also allows us to collectively mourn, immediately—sending lightning-fast, entirely impermanent notes of condolence, to no one and everyone, into the ether. The stages of grief online are a quick and immediate flurry. It happens often, as our cultural heroes age and die. When they've lived past eighty, as Andy Griffith did, we typically celebrate their contributions and mark full lives rather than truly mourn. Yet there I was, headphones wrapped around my head, facing the reflective screen of my giant iMac, on a high floor in lower Manhattan, shedding real tears for a man I never met, an actor.

In the following days, in Grand Rapids, Michigan, a young man named Sam Cook-Parrott gathered a group of musician friends and set down for eternity a lo-fi pop-punk tribute called "Andy Griffith." It's a catchy song, with a simple, infectious, wailing melody. Cook-Parrott calls his band Radiator Hospital, and its six-minute EP,

Some Distant Moon, was released on November 2, 2012. Sam wrote, "The song is about when the deaths of cultural figures/childhood idols affect you more than the actual relationships you have with people in your life." It's a remarkable song—created by someone who graduated high school in 2009 and who wrote on his blog that he's never been west of Minnesota or south of Maryland and, until recently, when he moved to Philadelphia, had not been out of Michigan for more than two weeks. "The night Andy Griffith died I just stayed around, I just stayed around." What Sam Cook-Parrott likely experienced was what I and a host of others felt—real grief.

I don't know the context of Cook-Parrott's grief, but as to mine? Betty Lynn was right. Andy Griffith was a surrogate father. Cable arrived in our neck of North Carolina in the 1980s, a few years after my father was killed. My older sister, as a precocious eleven-year-old, matched our family's blood types and discovered our newly dead father couldn't have contributed to my DNA. Things in the house got even worse after that.

But on cable, *The Andy Griffith Show* aired three or four times daily out of stations in Chicago and Atlanta, in addition to our local CBS station in nearby Greensboro. Toggling between episodes was thrilling; I usually lingered on the superior early seasons filmed in black and white, especially those that gave Don Knotts's character, Deputy Barney Fife, the most screen time. Mom would slam and lock her bedroom door; we could hear her throw open the drawers of her cherrywood nightstand, a metronomic ticking of brass handles answering each push and pull. We'd hear the vial of pills rattle and

Mom loudly counting out the number of Darvon capsules she had left, judging whether there were enough to cause certain death rather than a coma. When this happened, I'd turn up the volume of *The Andy Griffith Show*.

When Andy Griffith died I had an almost Pavlovian memory of myself as a lonely child bounding indoors when I heard *The Andy Griffith Show*'s whistling theme music. It is a curious thing about grief that mixed in with our sadness is the knowledge of our own mortality, the loss of who we once were. As Gerard Manley Hopkins wrote in the final couplet of "Spring and Fall," which he composed as a young country priest in Wales, "It is the blight man was born for, / It is Margaret you mourn for." I mourn for the boy who could lose himself in Mayberry—in half-hour stints I existed outside of time—braver, lighter.

20.

In a 1972 interview, Frances Bavier credited Andy Griffith with making the show what it was—believable—especially to the people of North Carolina, where she moved, sight unseen, that same year. She said Andy didn't structure the show but paid attention to everything, and if things weren't right, he'd help fix it and pepper in details from his experience. Bavier, who played Aunt Bee, was reclusive in her last decades, pestered by fans, like my high school girlfriend Lynn, who once put a cigarette out on my arm and who with her friends would sneak up on Bavier's house late at night, bang on a window, and then race away in an '81 Camaro. On Frances Bavier's Siler City tombstone, under her given name and the dates she existed on earth, carved in the stone it reads, "Aunt Bee," and underneath, "To live in the hearts of those left behind is not to die." A North Carolina couple purchased Bavier's Studebaker for $20,000 at the estate auction in 1990, a year after her death, the profits bequeathed to North Carolina public television—the Studebaker had four flat tires and Bavier's cats had ruined its interior. She also left a financial legacy for the local police department, in gratitude for the many times they chased teenagers away from her windows.

Fans often note that Bavier and Andy weren't close. That Bavier was difficult. Howard Morris, who played Ernest T. Bass on the show, referred to Bavier with fondness, as a "great old Broadway broad." Meaning old Broadway. Bavier was raised in New York City, growing up in a fine house in Gramercy Park; her father, Charles, was a respected engineer and held the responsibility for maintaining a feat of ingenuity, the Metropolitan Life Insurance Company Tower, off Madison Square Park. The Gothic Revival skyscraper was the tallest in the world when it was built and held the honor until the Woolworth Building rose downtown in 1913. Frances had a sensitive nature, and Andy knew this, which is why, after the first day of shooting on *The Andy Griffith Show* and Danny Thomas had raised his voice, yelling at Bavier, Andy had Danny Thomas banned from the set, knowing full well that Thomas owned an equal percentage of the show.

It is of note that a series written by World War II veterans, who fought jackbooted fascism, would create Barney Fife, who loves his uniform, his shiny bullet, his authority, and the letter of the law far too much, and we laugh at him. He's hilarious. Keeping Barney in check is our hero, Andy Taylor, a man who cares for his neighbors and disdains power over others. When Andy leaves town, Barney puts the entire community in jail. When he returns, Andy sets them free. Humanism triumphs over authority.

When they were little, my two children's favorite episode was "Opie and the Bully." When it aired in 1961, the writer credited was David Adler. David Adler was the name used by Brooklyn-born, Oscar-winning screenwriter Frank Tarloff, who wrote nine episodes for *The Andy Griffith Show*. Tarloff had been an uncooperative witness when called before the House Un-American Activities Committee in 1953, at the height of McCarthyism—Tarloff refused to name names. He was immediately fired from his job as a writer on the NBC sitcom *I Married Joan*, dropped from his talent agency, and blacklisted. Frank Tarloff knew something of bullies. (Spoiler: Opie wins, and each time this happens, my kids jump up and shout with joy.)

21.

Mount Airy had its Graceland moment in the early 1990s when the mayor and local businesspeople decided to capitalize on the stream of pilgrims wandering in Snappy Lunch and asking after Andy Griffith. In 1990, the *Atlanta Journal-Constitution* reported, "Among Mount Airy business leaders, such meager attention to what they view as a potential windfall in Mayberry tourism is like watching a river of gold flow out to sea." The mayor at the time, Maynard Beamer, told the paper, "Some of us would like to set up a place and call it Mayberry, maybe between here and the interstate." Later that year, the *Washington Post* covered the first Mayberry Days celebration, quoting the Surry Arts Council director Tanya Jackson:

> Mount Airy being the inspiration for [Mayberry] felt it would like to do something, anything, in honor of the show and for any Andy Fans who might be making a pilgrimage to The Birthplace.

The corporeal town reimagined as a fiction, the fiction a shadow version of the town. Portraits in convex mirrors.

Mount Airy is not the only town to celebrate *The Andy Griffith Show*. Westminster, South Carolina, almost 300 miles southwest of Mount Airy, toward Atlanta, began its own Mayberry Days, replete with antique replica Mayberry sheriff's cars and actors portraying characters from the show on parade. In towns in Indiana, Georgia, Ohio, and elsewhere, fans of the show gather. There is a May-berry Cruise to the Caribbean each summer.

The evening of September 23, 2012, during the "In Memoriam" section of the primetime Emmy Awards tele-cast, we witnessed an industrial acknowledgment of the importance of Andy Griffith, who had passed away less than three months prior. In the planning of the broadcast, there was contention over how many seconds of screen time to dedicate to the actor, as there were dozens of other well-respected recently dead to celebrate, including Harry Morgan, Dick Clark, Don Cornelius, Phyllis Diller, Sherman Hemsley, Celeste Holm, Ben Gazzara, Ernest Borgnine, Mike Wallace, and Andy Rooney, among others. In a tightly run awards show—banter, description, win-ning announcements, thirteen-pound statues of metal placed in the hands of the living—such a thing demands attention. The clock is ticking. *The Andy Griffith Show* opening appeared on the giant screen above center stage. Ron Howard walked slowly from upstage, surrounded by giant electronic displays of Andy Griffith, approached the microphone, and spoke for a full one minute and twen-ty-seven seconds, over 120 words, among them:

I was able to grow up professionally in that collab-orative, fun, but hard-working environment that was defined by Andy's tastes, his creative energy, his unwavering respect for the audience, and the unique possibilities that he believed our show could offer. Andy's legacy of excellence, accessi-bility, and range, puts him in the pantheon . . ."

Not the pantheon of great actors, or pantheon of shows, simply the "pantheon"—all the gods of a people. Howard then introduced the traditional "In Memoriam" montage (which did *not* include the other *Andy Griffith Show* star who died in 2012, George "Goober" Lindsey). The statement this tribute made was profound, like an ornamental gated plot at a cemetery—here was a remarkable man deserving of exceptional appreciation.

In stark contrast to the Emmys, during the three-minute "In Memoriam" segment of the Academy Awards broadcast on February 24, 2013, Andy Griffith was conspicuously absent. The eighty-fifth Oscars ceremony was mired in controversies, ranging from criticism leveled at its makers for an excess of Broadway-style song and dance numbers, to organized protest of the adolescent humor of host Seth MacFarlane, to outrage over an unfunny and ill-conceived comment about a child actor posted on Twitter and then deleted by the satirical newspaper *The Onion* (its publisher later publicly apologized). Yet the perceived snub of Andy Griffith was reported in several major news outlets the following day, including the *New York Times*, *Slate*, the *New York Daily News*, *Huffington Post*, and CNN. Other deceased actors were left out of the memorial montage, but it was Andy Griffith's name used in every headline, accompanied by an unsmiling photo. The outrage was widespread online—on social media, on blogs, in comments sections of news outlets, wherever people now express themselves. One YouTube user shakily captured the memorial segment with a hand-held camera, as it appeared on his TV, and then posted the footage without comment and the spare title "Andy

Griffith Missing." Griffith had appeared in eleven feature films—the more critically acclaimed were Adrienne
Shelly's *Waitress* (2007) and Howard Zieff's *Hearts of the
West* (1975)—but most of the anger was for *not* acknowl-
edging Griffith's starring role in Elia Kazan's *A Face in the
Crowd*. Film and television director Peyton Reed was still
sore about it the next day when he wrote via Twitter, "It
was a bummer not seeing the great Andy Griffith in the 'In
Memoriam' tribute last night. *A Face in the Crowd* is in my
all-time top ten." Reed told London's *Telegraph* in 2003,
"*A Face in the Crowd* is Elia Kazan's forgotten movie. The
LA Times and the *New York Times* barely mentioned it in
their recent obituaries [of Kazan]. It might not be his best
film, but for me it's his most fascinating."

The week following the Oscar broadcast, to show its
disdain for the Academy's omission of Andy Griffith,
NBC affiliate WKYC-TV in Cleveland broadcast a 1992
Matlock movie, preempting two hours of contemporary
programming: the sitcoms *The Office* and *1600 Penn* and
the drama *Law & Order: SVU*.

In 1957, Andy and his wife Barbara spoke from their
New York City apartment with Edward R. Murrow on
his weekly CBS interview show, *Person to Person*. The
first thing Murrow asks, in his iconic newsman baritone,
is, "Well, Andy, as one Tar Heel to another, when do you
expect to go home again?" Murrow, too, was raised poor in
North Carolina, living as a child in a cabin without plumb-
ing or electricity along the banks of the impossibly named
Polecat Creek, outside of Greensboro. There's a moment
just before Andy answers Murrow's question when the
expression in each of their eyes, Andy's and Barbara's,

together with Murrow's, shows that they know that Murrow is alluding to North Carolina's Thomas Wolfe and his last novel, *You Can't Go Home Again,* published posthumously by Scribner in 1940.

> You can't go back home to your family, back home to your childhood . . . back home to a young man's dreams of glory and of fame . . . back home to the places in the country . . . away from all the strife and conflict of the world, back home to the father you have lost and are looking for, back home to someone who can help you, save you, ease the burden for you, back home to the old forms and systems of things which once seemed everlasting but which are changing all the time—back home to the escapes of Time and Memory.

Some orbiting subatomic particles of Thomas Wolfe are zooming between them as Andy Griffith answers Murrow with a giant smile, saying he'd just bought a place in Manteo, on Roanoke Island—the same North Carolina acreage where he would die and be buried fifty-five years later. Manteo is the first location of English settlement in the New World, Sir Walter Raleigh's failed attempt to bring English civilization to a perceived wilderness. For the settlers of Andy's beloved Lost Colony, the wilderness won.

In Mayberry, Thelma Lou didn't put a cigarette out on Barney's arm like my girlfriend did to me; Andy Taylor wasn't embittered or slump-shouldered after a lifetime of ridicule by those with more social status. Still, Mayberry was a believable universe without these things.

Tools of television helped make this true—camera angles, lighting, a disciplined laugh track, extras so far in the background they are almost invisible, along with other aspects—but there is one thing about the story that has not been discussed, and it is the thing that gives it gravitas and why I, and others, watched. Opie's mother is dead, unaccountably, before the show begins—it's what sets the fiction in motion. Aunt Bee arrives to keep Opie from growing up wild and sullen—to keep the home from falling apart. The show offers humor to contend with a constant state of grief.

In 1963, Andy Griffith appeared on Bob Hope's NBC comedy special, invited to lampoon *The Andy Griffith Show*. In the ten-minute sketch, Hope, as the nation's Mafia boss, arrives in Mayberry to create an alibi for a high-profile murder. Hope brings with him a parade of violence, sex, extortion, racketeering, and ill-gotten riches. In the end, all the players, including Andy, are piled dead on the floor, shot in a battle of rival gangs. After a beat, Andy slowly rises, grabs his fishing rod, and makes for the door. Bob Hope lifts his head, "Hey, Andy, wait a minute, you're supposed to be dead. Where ya going?" Andy answers, "Fishing. On my show we always have a happy ending."

The small town where I grew up in North Carolina was not so unlike Andy Griffith's hometown of Mount Airy. It was a dry county. Churches were prominent. We had a sole high school that the community rallied around. Still, in this little idyllic town, the dad next door beat his sons without mercy; a lady down the street shot her drunken husband; a teenager fell into a coma after tumbling off his skateboard and fracturing his skull; a state trooper's son, just out of high school, offered all us boys playing kick-the-can a dollar if we'd let him give us blow jobs; the dentist's son shot himself in the chest; the coroner's son hung himself; the dad I'd known was long dead, my natural father forever estranged, my mother silent behind her bedroom door, trapped by depression and prescription narcotics. When I heard that famous whistling theme song at 5:30 p.m., I ran inside, knelt on the floor, and turned my face fully toward the screen. I came inside when I was called.

22.

When I first moved to New York City from North Carolina, I had to teach myself not to smile and nod at everyone I passed on the sidewalk. For months, all the faces I'd seen during the day flew past me again, and I'd smile and nod at each of them before I fell asleep. After fifteen years, if I was close to my apartment building, the chances were good I had met the person I was passing, so I smiled and nodded if I felt like it. I found NYC a warm and engaging place, magical and energizing. I was active physically—running and biking in the park, walking everywhere—and active culturally. I attended plays, movies, and art exhibits, usually on purpose, and kept abreast of all that was happening, despite not always having the time or money to see whatever was happening *as* it was happening. But it was important that I knew that it was happening and that I intended to witness it before it was forgotten and lost. I had friends at work and friends in the neighborhood, and we saw each other whether we liked it or not. I met old friends from North Carolina, scattered all over town, for drinks, or lunch, or dinner, on a steady basis, or once every few years, or just once, or at least made plans, or talked about making plans. Weekly invitations arrived for events and gatherings. I mostly didn't go to these events, but it was enough to be invited. As I worked in the publishing industry, there were always book parties and readings and sometimes actual party-parties that I wanted to be invited to and intended to go to but then did not attend. I felt plugged in. I often stopped at the Bowery Hotel or the

Ace to charge my phone. I had family memberships at the New Museum on the Bowery and the Central Park Zoo. I ran along the East River to work and home four times a week and walked the other days, which was my favorite half hour. I'd vary my route to pass different parts of Chinatown or Little Italy or the many micro-neighborhoods that populate downtown. I had a wonderful life. When my marriage ended abruptly after fifteen years and my ex moved to Massachusetts with my kids, I quit my job, borrowed money from friends and family, and tried to build a new life in New England.

I left Lower Manhattan for a garage apartment on a small farm, knowing no one in New England, and barely began a career as a freelance writer—with no savings, no freelance sea legs, no long list of editor contacts, no contracts to speak of, no steady paydays. I worked as a live-in hired man for a young professional family. They were nice enough people. The man drove a Prius and ran a company that made it easier for people to plan and purchase travel experiences on their phones. And the woman was an expert on psychological trauma at Harvard. I picked up their two kids from soccer once a week, and that was the extent of our interaction. There was a barn full of chickens, an asshole of a white rooster named Sunny, a cow and a bull in the meadow. The cow was expecting a calf. The original part of the main house dated to the seventeenth century. The foundation of the garage was dated 1998, the last year of *Seinfeld*, with a previous family's small handprints in the concrete. Yet, typical of New Englanders, the builders matched the architectural details and used reclaimed wood, so the feel of the structure was very much of the colonial era that, for some reason, New Englanders fetishize to the point of caricature. The interior of the apartment was comfortable and airy and very much of the "Must See TV" era in its choice of countertop and cabinets, like the *Seinfeld* apartment, but the door pulls, window frames, and wide plank floors all screamed 1775. Despite the intense winters of New England, the new windows on the 1998 building were designed in the 1775 style, handcrafted, using eighteenth-century tools, with rough-carved wooden winter window frames stored in a crawl space and wooden slots fitted for each, painted sad gray. Each frame was marked with chalk or tape indicating where it belonged. This was one of my tasks: to install the colonial windows in my 1998 replica outbuilding, and in the main house as well. I talked about my divorce as I installed the windows. The woman nodded and pretended to listen but was wise not to respond to anything I said, or I would have kept talking. I also cleaned the giant barn that was rolled down from somewhere in Maine. The previous owner owned horses. I noticed some of the old tack as I was mucking out the chicken shit.

Running along Main Street, I decided my way out of this mess was to write a book about a huge swath of American culture from the postwar era on to the present day, touching on ideas about fatherhood and masculinity, class prejudice, regionalism, racism, southernness, the folk revival, Hollywood, McCarthyism, the American dream. And this book would also be, most of all, about Andy Griffith. I'd use Andy's life and career as a tether, to weigh myself to earth, to keep from floating into the stratosphere, from spinning out of our Andy Griffith planet's rotational gravity and moving forever in space, never to be heard from again. And I'd meet people. I'd speak with people. I'd travel. I'd see the country. I'd make this new world in Massachusetts, where I knew no one at all, less lonely. And to help support this endeavor, to earn money, I'd find stories for magazines, profile some of the people I'd speak with, actors and directors, my new friends; I'd write about them for glossies and discuss their current film projects and earn a nice freelance payday all while completing my big book about a huge swath of American culture in the postwar era. I'd turn in the book in nine months or a year, get paid, and write a new book proposal for my next book about some other quirky idea that I'd already mapped out.

Some schemes for books I came up with included "A World History of Barbecue" and "The Hotel Lobby Bars of Earth." I also had been writing children's books with my kids, one called "The Adventures of Guh and Stick," after my oldest's imaginary friends when he was in preschool. Stick was a tree monster. Guh was a robot. I couldn't decide which book I wanted to do next. One of those. "The Hotel Lobby Bars of Earth" would take me to all the places I've always wanted to visit and would allow me to revisit some of my favorite bars, mostly back in NYC. But then again, world history—barbecue. Anyway, I'd spend the rest of my newly single life traveling and meeting people and writing books and magazine stories about them when I wasn't home taking care of my kids on the divided custody days. Days I'd had to fight for in court, the lawyers yelling at each other in the hallway. When my thoughts stopped racing even for a moment, I could still see the saliva streaming out of my ex-wife's lawyer's tiny mouth.

Such a small man. A bully. He tried to break my hand when I met him and had a penchant for kicking his foot up and pretending to tighten the shoelace on his small, shiny black pointed derby shoes, positioned against my thigh, when I was sitting alone on a cold wooden bench in those awful halls. I hated him. I hated the whole ugly process. These were the images that glanced across my mind when I had moments to think about my Andy Griffith book. Andy Griffith was married three times and divorced twice. His second wife, Solica, quit acting and became a family therapist. Maybe I'd write a book about divorce in America. About what a racket it is. People mercilessly bilking the vulnerable and afraid. Either way, I needed to finish my Andy Griffith book before I could do anything else. I had a plan. A way forward. As I ran along Main Street, it was clear and in front of me. One step leading to the next.

23.

This is the Michael Jordan's number of chapters.

24.

Several years have passed since this book about a wide swath of American culture tethered by the life and career of Andy Griffith began its long and difficult passage from concept to completion. At various moments during those years it seemed impossible, and at other times it seemed within reach—merely an adjusting of a few paragraphs, an outpouring of accumulated thoughts, and the book would be done. In the first months after the contract was signed, when I should have initiated a flurry of writing, I had recently left my marital home in Lower Manhattan, where I'd lived for the better part of twenty years, and found myself in that bachelor's garage apartment on a farm in Massachusetts, about fourteen miles west from where my ex-wife had suddenly moved. On days I wasn't with my kids, I wanted to travel on short reporting trips to California, and Arkansas, and research my book, and I did burn through cash on several reporting trips, yet I could not afford to travel nearly as much as I had hoped, since I had left my job in New York City in an attempt to stay close to my children amid this aggressive divorce. Most of the time, I could barely afford food for myself and gas for the car. I researched and plotted on the Internet, although much of that research was punctuated by pacing the wide plank floors of my garage apartment, yelling into my phone that all this back-and-forth had ruined my life, as I received weekly calls from my NYC lawyer to remind me that the divorce had destroyed my life. I'd repeat back what the lawyer said, and she'd repeat back what I yelled, and then she'd send a bill for $400 for this important phone call that I could not pay for.

Reeling, spiraling, Monday morning, I'd sit down at the kitchen counter to write. The eighty-dollar TV I bought at a Target on Route 9 was my only friend in Massachusetts. I did not find New England a friendly or welcoming place. I'd walk the half-mile to Stop & Shop for Cape Cod potato chips, a dozen eggs, and a half-case of Whale's Tail Pale Ale in cans, and then not leave the house until it was my turn to pick the kids up from school the following Friday. I'd have my kids for a few days, and everything would be normal and happy, sunlight and fresh air. I'd stock the fridge with real food and make cheese omelets and fry bacon for breakfast and prepare big bowls of pasta for dinner. We'd watch Marvel movies, like the *Avengers* and *Ant-Man*, who is my favorite Avenger for a bunch of reasons, largely because his story starts as a down-on-his-luck divorced dad, torn from his child, whom he loves more than anything in the world. On the weekends with my kids, we'd read books and watch *The Andy Griffith Show*, and then I'd drive them to school Monday morning, cursing and dumbfounded by the design of the roads—the short on-ramps and off-ramps, and winding weird paths, and sudden traffic, and traffic circles—and then I'd repeat the weekly process. Nine months later I moved. Then I moved again. Then I gave up on New England and moved two and a half hours away to the Hudson Valley, where I had a few friends who cared about whether I lived or died, and I thought I could commute from the Hudson Valley to NYC and regain a potential career. Then, almost immediately after this move, an accident on I-84 stopped traffic and I missed my son's soccer game, and I realized moving to the Hudson Valley—where I knew people, and strangers were friendly, and it was closer to Manhattan—was a terrible mistake, and as soon as I could manage it, I moved back to Massachusetts, this time with almost nothing, seventy bucks in my pocket and a half a tank of gas, again as a live-in hired man for a great artist couple and their cool eight-year-old kid, and on the day I arrived, I drove to the nearest coffee shop and asked where the closest decent restaurant was and the best grocery store. Still a New Yorker, I expected the best, but in this instance I was simply broke and alone and needed a job that same day, and within an hour I walked in both places, the restaurant and the store, with my standard ragged wool sport coat, looking like a downtrodden professor, and, as a middle-aged father of two, with a graduate degree from an Ivy League school, landed two low-wage jobs, waiting tables at the restaurant and clerking at the grocery store. And I was grateful. I worked evenings and during the day did light chores around the house and once or twice a week picked up my patrons' kid from school or soccer and made him mac and cheese. Then, a year after that, I moved still again, finally, to the North Shore of Massachusetts, a truly gorgeous and far friendlier place than anything I'd before encountered in New England. The North Shore seemed a newly discovered paradise. People sometimes even said hello and smiled when I passed them on the street.

All this time, I couldn't focus on pitching stories to magazines, as I have only one or two of what I think are good ideas in a calendar year, and I feared freelance stories would take time away from the Andy Griffith book, which by this point, in fits and starts, was about 50,000 words and represented enough research to fill the back of a lime-green 1934 Ford pickup, or any of the other cars in Andy Griffith's antique car collection. He also owned a 1930 Model A, a 1938 Buick Special, and another Buick convertible, a 1928 Ford Phaeton. Andy collected cars, watches, and hats—all the things a poor kid growing up in a mill town in the 1930s would have wanted—to give himself status.

One Andy Griffith expert posited that, since Andy never purchased a yearbook photo, he didn't enjoy his days at the University of North Carolina, but this "expert" neglected to take into account that a yearbook photo cost almost four dollars and Andy couldn't afford it. He was a scholarship student. A worker. Single-minded.

I knew these things, and they bounced around my head all the time. When my mates at the store asked me how the book was going, I'd usually say, "Oh, I have about 50,000 words, but it's mostly all the same word."

For the few assignments I'd been given early on by magazines, I missed the deadlines, or never wrote the pieces, putting them off until inevitably the editors moved to another publication, which in the magazine industry is every few weeks. One I didn't write, about the history of one-camera sitcoms, was for *Slate*; another short piece I never wrote about TV father figures was for *Time*; and another I sadly was too distracted by my divorce to write, even after accumulating tons of research, was about the richness of North Carolina cultural landmarks in New York City, like a Manhattan shop where Andy Griffith's pal Gene McLain, an actor who played Governor White in

The Lost Colony, sold art, jewelry, and furniture he made from driftwood and other natural objects he collected from Roanoke Island and the beach at Nags Head. It was for a North Carolina magazine called *Our State*. The editor and I were from the same town in North Carolina and had gone to the same skating rink as kids: Jones Skating Rink in Randolph County, where I experienced my first real kisses the summer before sixth grade. All us kids were outside, leaning against the cinder block wall, lit by the yellow glow of the streetlight high on a telephone pole, with swarms of mosquitoes and moths floating in the haze, being picked off by dozens of bats. We all left the rink early, pretending to wait on our parents to pick us up, knowing they wouldn't come for another twenty-five minutes. When I missed the deadline, the editor stopped following me on Twitter. Choking in the smoke, I was afraid of burning more bridges, so stopped pitching stories and hid behind my Andy Griffith book. I was lonely. Living in a strange town. Then another strange town. Then another. Then came the pandemic. I became a stranger to all, even to myself. To everyone except my kids, thank God.

Over these years, the remnants of my old life in Manhattan were slowly peeled away, or sold off to pay rent and child support. I actively sought better-paying work, applying and interviewing for jobs, daily, but I did not find a job in New England in my field (it was as if I no longer understood how the world functioned outside Manhattan). I worked full-time at first in a bistro and then finally at a grocery store, where I was paid to speak with people, and they were forced by nature of the social pact inherent in our shared commerce to speak in some fashion with me, held captive by my ridiculous stories, anecdotes about either New York City or growing up in North Carolina. I timed these stories to last the duration of our three-minute encounter, the minutes it took to scan the barcodes on their purchases, place them in bags, take their money, and hand them their receipt and change. Sometimes customers laughed out loud, charmed by my southern manner, and sometimes they smiled uncomfortably as I poured a beer, told them the nightly specials, or bagged groceries. Eventually I landed a low-paying editorial gig for a local newspaper, tangentially in my field: the night shift, editing obituaries.

I worked in the grocery store during the day. Before the pandemic of 2020, it was sometimes fun, albeit backbreaking, humbling, and dirty work, crawling around on the dark, cold concrete floor in the dairy box, throwing cartons of eggs on the shelf. I learned to live with constant physical pain but felt good about myself most of the time, physically strong, well fed, and appreciated. I loved the store and the people who worked there and many of the customers, and I counted any day a good day that a customer didn't insult me. Most people are kind, but the ones who are not I'll likely remember the rest of my life. Like the guy who screamed at me, "Who do you think you are, some moron making minimum wage telling me what to do!" This was during the pandemic when the floor was marked where to stand, to maintain social distance, and all I could think to say was, "No one here makes minimum wage." And he jeered, "You don't deserve minimum wage." He waited until he was halfway across the parking lot when he yelled this. I had never owned a college class ring but ordered the cheapest one, and paid for it in installments, just to flash when a customer instructed me to "keep the cold items together" or "put the eggs on top." It was an eerie time, driving to work, no cars on the road, working the door just like I did at rock clubs in college, but instead of checking IDs, I was making sure people were wearing masks. I sometimes thought of Barbara Ehrenreich, who wrote *Nickel and Dimed*, recounting how after that book's success, people often said to her that she was brave for working low-wage jobs to report on class and economic status, and she'd answer, "What about the millions of people who do that every day and don't write about it?" As physical jobs go, working in a grocery store is not the absolute worst. For one long muggy North Carolina summer I loaded tractor trailers, and that was harder. Still, all of my coworkers at the store had sacrificed some part of their bodies for the wage—a back, a knee, a shoulder, an eye; some part of them had been permanently injured. And it was only with hazard pay during the pandemic that the store provided a living wage.

At night I edited the obits and death notices of New England's recently departed. Both jobs—at the grocery store and for the newspaper—gave me a better understanding of the place I was living in. I began to see the kindnesses and eccentricities of the region shine through. Its old beauty. I made note of how often an obituary made mention of the Red Sox or the Patriots—which was every single one. And sometimes the Celtics and the Bruins. But I'd little time left to do much else than work or make dinner for my kids, and while we ate we'd watch *The Andy Griffith Show* or another sitcom, like *The Office*,

Parks and Recreation, or *Bob's Burgers*. Greg Daniels, who had a strong hand in creating the American version of *The Office* and *Parks and Recreation*, began his career with Conan O'Brien, writing jokes for North Carolina–born Rich Hall on *Not Necessarily the News*. Daniels loves *The Andy Griffith Show*. As does Vince Gilligan, who gave the world Walter White and *Breaking Bad*. Mike Judge created *King of the Hill* with Daniels, an animated sitcom that features a put-upon, middle-aged Texas family man, Hank Hill. Judge said of Daniels, discussing Hank's character, "Greg had a line which I thought was pretty great, something like 'Andy Griffith is back and he's pissed off.'"

When I wasn't working at the grocery store or the newspaper, I was driving back and forth to see my kids or to pick my kids up or drop them off. And almost the entire time mired in ongoing litigation. When I had spare moments at home, I applied for better employment, as working all the time at those two jobs I (still!) barely had enough money for food and gas. But the bills were paid—at least most of the current ones. Still, the jobs, with notice, had flexible hours, and the supervisors understood the vagaries of shared custody and the life of a single parent. I also did odd jobs for cash payments for my landlord and for a few months was one of those fearless and intrepid servants of the people who knocked on doors with a lanyard around my neck and a U.S. government–issued smart phone in my hand, asking people how old they were and having doors slammed in my face. Yes, I was a census worker. With quarterly raises and hazard pay, by the middle of the pandemic I was finally earning almost enough to squeak by, but like most everyone considered an "essential worker," I was constantly afraid of dying simply by clocking in five days a week and then clocking out. Sometimes I'd hide in the deep freezer after a customer had gotten close to my face and taken off her mask to ask me where the French green beans were, or another licked his fingers before he handed me his money.

However, I had a plan. I spent so much of my time driving back and forth to work and to see my kids that for months I tried dictating notes on my book about Andy Griffith to Siri, my ancient phone's personal assistant. With the phone mounted on a magnetic station on the dash, my plan was to record thoughts and notes and also rough chapters of material. I intended to accumulate a ton of stories without thinking too much or stressing about it. I'd wait until I was at a good stopping point to listen to them and then read and edit the transcriptions. Say, after several months. During each trip in the car to pick up the kids, or after I dropped them off, my mind would open to this wide swath of American culture, rather than close to the mind-numbing grief of not being in the daily lives of my children, and I'd tell the story of "Looking for Andy Griffith."

Often after I delivered my kids to their mother's, I'd drive for hours, aimlessly, wandering the countryside, not wanting to return to my empty home. My life was lived largely absent of other people, as well as most of my belongings. One time, early on, after watching my kids run inside this new man's house where my ex-wife was living, I was so distraught that I drove straight for as long as possible, hour upon hour, fearing I'd get into an auto accident if I made a turn. I made a habit of this to cope with my grief.

It was a way of staying in the familiar car, with my kids' snacks and toys rattling in the backseat and juice stains on the headrests. I'd make only right turns if forced to stop and turn by a road ending at a perpendicular angle to another, maybe an older road leading to some older town. Other times, if I had my wits about me, I'd choose left. I'd not consult a map and kept the old dad wagon pointed west, or north, or northwest, depending on my mood. Even the names of the streets seemed weird and foreign, thanks to the Puritan naming conventions. In each of these little towns and bedroom communities, there was always a Concord Road, and a Pleasant Street, and a Sorrow Street, and Life Is Hardship Road, and Labor in Vain Road, and if you follow, say, Concord Road, it becomes Pleasant Street in the next town, and if you follow Pleasant Street, it eventually turns into Life Is Hardship Road, and when driving on any road in Massachusetts, one must know the name of the street you're driving on. If you do not know, you will never know, as each intersection has only one sign with one name, instead of two signs with two names. There are two streets, certainly, but one sign for one street is enough. The good people of Massachusetts have no interest in telling you where you are exactly, only what is next. It's as if the designers of the roads and byways of New England anticipated southern gothic fiction and had Flannery O'Connor in mind. "Where you come from is gone, where you thought you were going to never was there, and where you are is no good unless you can get away from it." Accustomed to my life walking the carefully measured street grid of Manhattan, an island swiped from the Lenape and flattened by the Dutch and laid out in 1811 by the New York City commissioners, I was permanently lost in New England.

After recording as I drove for months, I imagined I'd spoken into the recorder enough to start the work of listening through the dictation and gleaning the choice bits. I hoped I'd gathered some great stuff for my Andy Griffith book. I sorted through the initial menu of saved notes on my phone. The phone had automatically saved them by date and time; I had seen them adding up week by week. With each car trip to see my children or after delivering them back, I was building a narrative. There was a note for September 6 at 1 p.m. and another on September 8 at 4:35 p.m. Another on the thirteenth at 6:23 p.m. and on and on, each corresponding with the solo end of each trip I'd taken to ferry my kids between their two homes. Then, as I was excited with the idea of the fullness and richness of material and was finally ready to gather the transcriptions and build them into a coherent chapter, the first note I opened read only, "Siri, take a note ..." followed by a lot of nothing. An empty screen. The blank page. Silence. That was all. Each note with its own time stamp, its own file. "Siri, take a note . . ." "Take a note. Take a note . . ." The great nothing. Other entries, instead of "Take a note," read, "Rake denote." Laughing about it and in good cheer, knowing the material was bouncing around my frontal lobe, I downloaded a new dictation app and switched to that for a few weeks instead of using Siri. I could see it was recording and working, but I'd wait until I dictated enough material to make a dent in the manuscript. Again, I waited until I had delivered enough on those ambling car rides, snaking down old post roads and cow paths in New

England. One transcription began, "Molouf the other Aindlee Griffindor and watching eggs except national intro rain." And so on. Sentence after sentence. "Sorry, rake denote. Calabrian olives in parson shoes join which like euro contracts in diesel honey baked harm." All the dictation was far removed from human understanding. I could not parse my original meaning. Yet I was giddy with joy and optimism. My big important book, "Looking for Andy Griffith," in which I'd examine a wide swath of American culture in the postwar era and cast a gimlet eye on class, ethnicity, work, fatherhood, and comedy, was on its way. "Sorry, rake denote. Calabrian olives in parson shoes join which like euro contracts in diesel honey baked harm."

25.

Andy leaned against the black wrought-iron railing on the balcony; with one hand he gripped the top and tested its strength. He lit a cigarette with the butt end of the one he'd just been smoking. The party was only for the cast. His wife Barbara stayed home in their apartment across town. Dick was who knows where— probably Jilly's on West Fifty-Second. At this dinner party it was just the players in *A Face in the Crowd*, except Patsy's tall-ass Brit writer husband, Roald, holding court and acting like a jerk with the rest of them about all their culture and his lack. He didn't want to go back inside. Andy could see the dark expanse of Central Park in the near distance and the skyline of the East Side beyond it. If he leaned over the balcony to the right he could see the giant buildings of midtown, including the one where the William Morris office was located, its top flashing MONY, MONY.

He got it. Patsy had let him in on the game. Gadge had instructed them to make him feel unwelcome, stupid. Ignore him. Dismiss him. With everything he said, they acted like it was a miracle he strung enough words together to complete a sentence. The only one who acted the same, as always, was Budd.

PHI MU ALPHA SINFONIA FRATERNITY OF AMERICA

I Andrew Griffith do agree to pay to the alpha Rho chapter of Phi Mu alpha the sum of $10.00 this day December 1, 1945; and thereafter the sum of $5.00 by January 31, 1946 and $5.00 by February 28, 1946 to thus make the total sum of $20.00 that I shall pay to said alpha Rho chapter of Phi Mu alpha for initiation fees.

signed — Andrew Griffith

accepted — Joseph W. Marshall

Treasurer for Phi Mu alpha

December 1, 1945

Paid "1/19/46

Joseph W. Marshall

In 1945, Andy arranged to pay his Phi Mu Alpha Sinfonia Fraternity initiation fee on an installment plan, paying in full fourteen months after joining. Andy signed his name on the contract "Andrew."

ANDREW GRIFFITH
President

Mr. Griffith has natural leadership qualities and he is a person
well liked by everyone. Also his character is excellent. He is
very well equipped to teach vocal work (chorus and glee clubs)
but is only fair in instrumental work. The reason for this is
that only recently did he decide to prepare himself in instrumental music. I believe he has the ability to do a good job of
teaching in both vocal and instrumental but felt that he should
spend more time in the study of wind instruments. This could
probably be done in summer school. With his natural ability I
would not hesitate having him as a teacher for I know he will
"grow" in his work.

Music

April 9, 1949

A program headshot of Andy Griffith from his lead role in the
Carolina Playmakers 1949 production of Gilbert & Sullivan's *H.M.S.
Pinafore*. Courtesy of UNC–Chapel Hill Department of Dramatic
Art Photographs and Related Materials, Wilson Special Collections
Library, UNC–Chapel Hill.

BARBARA *and* ANDREW GRIFFITH
rehearse a skit

Barbara performed interpretive dances as part of their act while Andy sang folk songs and accompanied on guitar, ca. 1952.

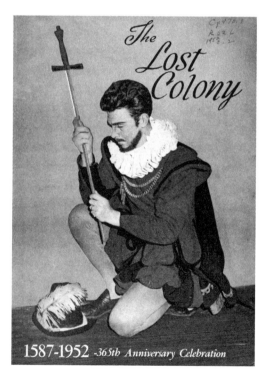

The Lost Colony 1952 season program cover, with Andy as the famed explorer, pirate, poet, and flawed court favorite Sir Walter Raleigh.

ANDREW GRIFFITH, *Sir Walter Raleigh*

This will be Andy's seventh season with *The Lost Colony*, his fifth as Sir Walter. Majoring in music at the University of North Carolina, he appeared in many dramatic roles with the Playmakers including *The Gondoliers, The Bartered Bride, The Mikado, H.M.S. Pinafore* and the leading role in *Egypt Lan'*. After doing music and drama work in the Goldsboro High School for several years he has for the past winter season acted with his wife, Barbara, (*Eleanor Dare of The Lost Colony*) in their own entertainment team throughout North and South Carolina and Virginia.

BARBARA EDWARDS GRIFFITH, *Eleanor Dare*

She is the first native North Carolinian to play the female lead of the drama and this is her sixth season as Eleanor Dare. Her acting and singing career started at Converse College, Spartanburg, S. C. Later she studied at the University of North Carolina where she appeared in *The Beggar's Opera* and *Egypt Lan'*. She has also done concert work in the two Carolinas, and during the past winter teamed with her husband Andy Griffith of *The Lost Colony* cast in sponsoring themselves in a successful entertainment career. Due to her excellent voice and splendid acting ability she has been the most successful actress to portray the difficult role of *Eleanor Dare*.

TOP

From the 1953 *The Lost Colony* program. After only months as a full-time entertainer, Andy's career would skyrocket that November, and on January 10, 1954, Andy was booked on *The Ed Sullivan Show*.

BOTTOM

Andy Griffith performing at Kenan Stadium, September 25, 1954. Photograph by Hugh Morton, courtesy of the North Carolina Collection Photographic Archives, Wilson Library, University of North Carolina at Chapel Hill.

Andy reunites with his former record producer, Orville Campbell (wearing a Tar Heel tie), during a 1956 press meeting hosted by the social group Honorary Tar Heels at the University Club in New York City. Photograph by Hugh Morton, courtesy of the North Carolina Collection Photographic Archives, Wilson Library, University of North Carolina at Chapel Hill.

Andy Griffith and photo essayist Joe Clark at the 1956 Honorary Tar Heels press meeting. Joe Clark was an Honorary Tar Heel; Andy was an actual Tar Heel. Photograph by Hugh Morton, courtesy of North Carolina Collection Photographic Archives, Wilson Library, University of North Carolina at Chapel Hill.

Andy Griffith signing autographs at the 1958 Azalea Festival
in Wilmington, North Carolina. Photograph by Hugh Morton,
courtesy of the North Carolina Collection Photographic Archives,
Wilson Library, University of North Carolina at Chapel Hill.

The author's maternal grandmother, Sallie Dalton Simmons, with his mother, Betty, and her younger sister Brenda, in Mount Airy, North Carolina, mid-1940s. Courtesy of the author.

The author's maternal grandfather, Wallace Simmons, of Mount Airy, North Carolina, 1951. Courtesy of the author.

The author's mother, Betty Simmons Smith, ca. 1960. Courtesy of the author.

The author and his dad, Bob Smith, Nags Head, North Carolina, 1970. Courtesy of the author.

The author and his sister Logan,
early 1970s. Courtesy of the author.

The author and his sister Logan
at the Wright Brothers Memorial,
Kitty Hawk, North Carolina, 1970.
Courtesy of the author.

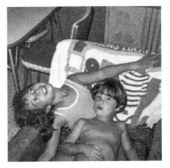

The author and his sister Logan at
a rented beach house on the Outer
Banks, early 1970s. Courtesy of
the author.

The author's locker at his grocery store job after he relocated from Manhattan to New England, 2017. Courtesy of the author.

Christmas 2022, Ipswich, Massachusetts. Living only a few blocks from the Ipswich River, the author and his children all surprised one another with gifts of fishing poles. Courtesy of the author.

26.

I've never been fishing. Not really. I didn't grow up close to water except for small rambling creeks or close to anyone who loved or knew the water, and when, in a fit of parenting when I was six or seven, my mother arranged for me to go lake fishing with a strange man I'd never met who volunteered through the Big Brothers program, I hid behind the dining hutch and didn't answer the door, duckwalking to the kitchen window and sneaking glimpses outside, when the well-meaning older man rang the doorbell. My mother was asleep in her room with the door locked or out running errands at the drugstore, I don't recall, but I do recall the man standing in denim coveralls, lingering by the garage door, scratching the back of his neck, before ringing the bell again, honking his car horn once more, and then rolling backward down the gentle incline of the white cement driveway in his tan Ford LTD, never to be seen again. As I think about this now, it would have made more sense for me to have met the man before he took me fishing. Perhaps I had, I don't recall, but in 1975, I'm not sure that my young, widowed mother considered it. When she learned I didn't answer the door, didn't want to go fishing, she never volunteered me for a Big Brother outing again. I never had a Big Brother. That day, I lay belly-down on the juice-stained tan carpet and watched *The Andy Griffith Show* on our RCA television. It came on one of three local stations the RCA dial received with tinfoil wrapped loosely around the balled end of each antenna. I watched the show every day. In the summertime, if I heard its whistling theme music, I'd know it was time to come in and wash up for dinner, as I'd been playing outside all day, barefoot and shirtless, like some imagined eighteenth-century frontier child. Each day, I watched the character Andy Taylor take his motherless son, Opie, fishing at Myers Lake. Andy walks hand-in-hand with his son, their fishing rods balanced across their shoulders. Opie stops to skip a rock across the lake.

My kids tell me they want to go fishing. I don't own any poles and don't have enough cash to buy any.

27.

Danville, Indiana, is an attractive small town, with red brick and white clapboard buildings and a walkable downtown. It sits within rolling hills on the outskirts of the sprawling metropolis of Indianapolis. On a clear day, under a pure blue sky in May, I approached a courtyard area near the town's center and saw a man from Mount Olive, North Carolina, Phil Fox, dressed as Ernest T. Bass, and also as late Elvis, wearing a gold cape.

The gathered crowd listened intently. Ticketed events featuring Maggie Peterson as Charlene Darling and the remaining members of the Dillards were indoors at the auditorium. My friend, whom I knew in high school, had driven with me from Ohio. Blonde and tan, with a toothy grin, she approached Ernest T. as Elvis after the performance, and he invited us back to the hotel where most of the performers and diehard *Andy Griffith Show* fans were staying. When we arrived, there were six replica Mayberry sheriff's cars in the parking lot, including one that had been fashioned from a golf cart. When we checked in our room and turned on the TV, my friend screamed. It was an episode of *The Andy Griffith Show*.

Later in the hotel lobby, a gathering of fans sat grouped together chatting and sipping on drinks in white Styrofoam cups. Some had driven from Ohio or Kentucky, others from outside Chicago. They knew one another as fans from attending Mayberry Days in North Carolina in years past. The youngest of them was fourteen, and he had won *The Andy Griffith Show* trivia contest from earlier in the day. I asked him which of the writers of the show were his favorite. He considered a moment, tilting his head slightly, and then said, "Ev Greenbaum and Fritzell."

"Mine too," I said.

An elderly gentleman with what looked like a war veteran's trucker hat—it actually said "Howard Sprague fan club" in gold thread on a blue background—nodded sagely, leaning back with his arms folded across his chest. The gentleman told me that he watched two episodes at once and wore special sunglasses to filter out other distractions, similar to blinders on a horse, so he could concentrate on gathering the details.

"We don't worship Andy Griffith," a woman said to me. "I mean, we love him, and love the show, but it's not a cult. It's about friendship. Over the years, going to Mayberry Days and other events, it's like seeing old friends."

MY FATHER IS GONE WILD INTO HIS GRAVE;
FOR IN HIS TOMB LIE MY AFFECTIONS,
AND WITH HIS SPIRITS SADLY, I SURVIVE,
TO MOCK THE EXPECTATION OF THE WORLD.

—Prince Hal, *Henry IV*, part 2, act 5, scene 2

28.

My life was in shambles. Shambles is one word for it. Train wreck. Hot mess. Implosion. Disarray. Destroyed. Lots of these words were used by kind friends to describe my situation. "Jesus Christ, Evan," my friend Michael said. "How are you able to go on? Many men in your situation would have killed someone or stuck a gun in his mouth. You're doing great. Things will get better. Things are getting better. Eventually they will get better. One day soon things will be better. Are you dating?"

29.

In my old home in Massachusetts, there was a digital fireplace in the bedroom. It was placed inside the space created for the real fireplace, made of brick and mortar, built when the house was built. After that real fireplace went unused, the chimney cracked and unsafe for flame, the previous owner purchased the digital fireplace, complete with electric fan and heating vents, from a manufacturer in Japan, mounted it inside the fireplace flush to the wall, and hung drywall over the stone, painting the wall to match the rest of the room. At first the fireplace seemed strange and weird, with its glowing blue-white glass at the base and flickering digital flames, orange and red and white. The flames licked upward in a pattern that mimicked the random chaos of real flame, to the point that for a moment you'd wonder if it was a push-button gas fireplace rather than a digital facsimile. This is *The Andy Griffith Show*.

30.

Alternate:

There were two fireplaces in my former home in Massachusetts. One was a woodstove set into a fireplace. It was flush and attractive, black iron and enamel, glossy, the wood burning inside, glowing and hot. I stared at the embers and coals to relax on a cold night. It was beautiful. Left unattended, it could kill us all.

31.

Vader: Obi-Wan never told you
what happened to your father.

Skywalker: He told me enough!
He told me you killed him!

Vader: No, I am your father.

In our earliest stories, fathers are unknowable, vengeful tyrants. Cronus murders his father the sky and then eats his own children out of fear he'll suffer the same fate, which he does—at the hands of his youngest boy, Zeus, with the help of his brothers. Zeus tosses his son Hephaestus off Mount Olympus and swallows Athena's mother whole, just after Athena's conception. In the Garden of Eden, Yahweh walked between his two human children, invisible, angry, and condemning.

And in our modern myths—comic books—Superman's heroic father was killed by an exploding sun; Spider-Man, too, is orphaned, and his story is set in motion when the poor high school kid from Queens is orphaned a second time, by the murder of his Uncle Ben.

Often, our heroes are orphans, entirely alone in the world. Or as they reach adulthood, the mysteriously absent father turns out to be a god.

We have a complicated relationship with our fathers.

In the last century, we've created new mythologies via radio, television, and the movies. On television, in particular, the figures arrived inside the home, walking and talking across the screen. Children whose own fathers were either absent or scarred by the Depression or world war looked to their televisions. I've met many men who have told me this.

This was the case in my own family: both my parents' fathers served in World War II, were absent during the early years of their children's lives, and returned changed men, for the salvation of democracy, perhaps, but to the detriment of their children's emotional lives.

For many kids, they were able to turn to their television to look for a surrogate father, a stand-in. For me, Andy Griffith was the largest figure.

I was at a fundraiser for an artists' organization in New Hampshire called MacDowell. Early in the evening I met the guy who created the "Three Wolf Moon" shirt— an Internet sensation of 2009. It made me happy that the gentleman was supporting the arts. Later at the event, a man came up to me and said he heard I was writing a book about Andy Griffith. He said he was raised on *The Andy Griffith Show*—he had endured a miserable home life as a child; had been a lonely, scared kid; and had learned his first positive ideas about living in the world from the show. The man is a writer and wrote the screenplay for a film Tom Hanks starred in that is largely about a man trying to be a decent, brave person faced with a world of cruelty and grief.

32.

I've only vague memories of my dad, Bobby Lee Smith, before the overly medicated lady in a Buick hit his little VW Beetle head-on in 1973 and the steering wheel was shoved into his broad chest and crushed his heart.

My memories following his death are easily recalled and profoundly vivid, but the collection of images I have of him before he died I can count on one hand.

As the father of two children, I am keenly aware of the love he must have felt for me, of the influence his love and attention must have had in shaping my personality, but it was only after having kids—at thirty-six—did I understand this. When my kids were the ages my sister and I were when my father died, it felt like I'd loved them a lifetime, and I can't recall the world without them.

33.

Here are the memories I have of my dad, just to set them down one time:

1. Dad was slicing pepperoni at our orange kitchen counter—after my mother and sister were asleep. He was slicing the sausage and lifting it to his mouth on the knife blade. He gave me some to eat. It was delicious.

2. After I opened my chest with a rusty handlebar of my sister's hand-me-down bicycle, Dad placed antibiotic on my reverse-S-shaped bloody cut that ran the length of my torso.

3. The morning I refused to go to church—my clothes laid out on the bed—Dad came in and stood over me, slowly took his belt off and laid it beside my clothes, and let me know those were my two choices. I got dressed.

4. I remember him dead. His casket was open and sky blue. Carolina blue. I was asked to kiss him—instead I ran my finger across the sloping ridge of his dark hair. I built up my nerve to kiss him on the rouged cheek, but they had closed the casket—so I kissed the casket. The aged funeral director lost his professional decorum and broke down and cried. My mother was proud of this, I think, that our grief was that profound.

34.

In June of 2013, my wife of fifteen years demanded a divorce, and I felt as if I had been murdered or killed in a head-on collision. It was sudden and unexpected. To be removed from the daily lives of my children created a well of grief and despair in me that I didn't know could possibly exist.

35.

In 1998, the same year I was married in a ceremony held in a Brooklyn apartment (a converted storefront on Bushwick Avenue in an ancient two-story building that had been an auto parts store and, before that, a stable), an archaeologist teamed with a climatologist to answer an old mystery. The two scientists proposed a viable theory for why the first English settlement in North America in 1585—Roanoke, or the Lost Colony, in what's now coastal North Carolina—failed: the settlers had arrived during the worst growing season drought in almost a millennium. Core samples from local 800-year-old bald cypresses tell the story. The scientists pinpointed the severe drought to a three-year span by counting and measuring the thickness of the great tree's rings. Those same years also marked the arrival of the colony and their eventual disappearance.

36.

In 1970, on TV screens around the world, a VW Beetle raced in the dirt and dust herding cattle as if the little car were a cowboy on horseback. Howard Zieff, who ran a successful advertising agency in New York City, created and directed this TV commercial. My dad liked the commercial. He'd grown up on farmland outside Mount Airy, milking cows each morning. He liked cowboys and westerns as much as anybody. As a child, I was gifted chaps, spurs, hats, and plastic six-shooters. Zieff's commercial influenced my dad's decision to trade in his old Buick Skylark for a new tan Beetle in 1971. And Andy Griffith loved westerns—it was his favorite genre. For his whole life, if he passed an old western on TV, he'd stop what he was doing, sit down, and watch it.

Howard Zieff had a solid reputation, and for his second film, *Hearts of the West*, starring twenty-five-year-old Jeff Bridges, who'd been acting since he was a baby, Andy agreed to take on the role of Howard Pike. It was an interesting character, with some depth to the comedy and a bit of drama. The script possessed the kind of genre bending and humanity that Andy preferred. It was about a young, naive writer of western pulp fiction who falls backward into acting in the early days of cowboy movies. Filming began in 1974 in Los Angeles. Jeff Bridges remembers, "The mood on the set created by our director, Howard Zieff, was wonderful, light, and filled with enthusiasm for all the players."

Hearts of the West is an odd and interesting film. Rob Thompson wrote the script and went on to a long career, including a significant contribution to the critically acclaimed ensemble TV series *Northern Exposure* (1990). One can guess *Hearts of the West* fueled the Coen brothers' approach to scripts and filmmaking. In recent years, *Rolling Stone* film critic Bilge Ebiri described the film as "one of Bridges' most interesting takes on the Western." But for all its sophisticated humor, it has a touch of vaudeville. It's like a proto–Coen brothers film, with a not-as-good soundtrack. It's fun to watch, and in biographies it's mentioned as a top role for Andy Griffith, along with *A Face in the Crowd* and *Waitress*. The film has a stellar cast. Supporting Bridges are Alan Arkin and Blythe Danner, both of whom I'd pay fifteen bucks just to watch eat a sandwich. Andy's character, Howard Pike, a bit-part cowboy actor in the early days of talking film, is complicated and has more depth than he at first seems to have, once you scrub the trail dust off his rough surface. He is erudite, a once-successful writer, and desperate and broken. It's a good part for Andy, especially in the early 1970s, after the ignominy of two comeback shows failing in the same year; his aborted barbecue restaurant empire, which he wanted just to forget about; and his recent divorce from Barbara. Even in the best cases, divorce is devastating. With *Hearts of the West*, things were looking up. He was being cast as a heel. And getting away from that Mayberry sheriff's uniform hand-stitched by Nudie Cohn in North Hollywood. Jeff Bridges wrote to me, "*Hearts of the West* gave Andy the opportunity to do comedy with some darker edges to it. He played the part of Howard Pike, an aging actor doing Westerns, beautifully."

37.

There are two things I love about Andy Griffith in a crass and obvious way. The first is that he so profoundly succeeded at portraying his character—Andy Taylor—that the culture has been reshaped. Mount Airy has altered its geography to accommodate the crush of visitors seeking to commune with the spirit of Andy Griffith. The second thing that fascinates me about Andy Griffith is his almost complete failure.

If a person swallows the entirety of Andy Griffith's failures at once, like a drug—it's overwhelming—it would kill. His career launched with failure. He was rejected at his first major audition at a New Jersey playhouse, told he couldn't sing—or, rather, that his voice was too big for the stage, which was unpleasant to the ears. He believed the man. A favorite music professor of Andy's suggested he should earn a living tuning pianos. Andy concentrated on comedy. But after a hit record, Andy failed after he was invited to New York City, booked for four segments on *The Ed Sullivan Show*, and fired after one. Andy bombed his first major nightclub stint at the famed Blue Angel, starting the second night (the first night went well, as it was packed with his friends, including Ainslie Pryor, who brought his castmates from the Broadway show *The Caine Mutiny Court-Martial*, including James Garner and Henry Fonda, who whooped it up). His screen debut, *A Face in the Crowd*, was a commercial failure and ignored by the Academy; his second film, *No Time for Sergeants*, was only a modest success; and the third, *Onionhead*, flopped so badly he was put in film jail for decades. Andy turned to television because he was not offered film roles. It was here, on *The Andy Griffith Show*, that he met with wild success, yet his attempt to break back into the movies in 1969 failed miserably, and after only one effort, *Angel in My Pocket*, Andy destroyed a five-film contract with Universal rather than make any more bad movies. Universal wanted to pair him with his *Andy Griffith Show* costar Don Knotts, and Andy refused. He had no desire to be Dean Martin to Don's Jerry Lewis. He knew Dean Martin and spent time with him, and he understood the burden of dependence on a partner for work. In the 1970–71 broadcast season, Andy had the galling distinction of failing at two television series.

There is more failure. More failed series and pilots and the failed promise of introducing the world to North Carolina barbecue with a fast-food restaurant chain. Jerzy Kosiński promised Andy the role of Chauncey Gardner in *Being There* (1979), until Peter Sellers got wind of the part and then won an Oscar for it. So Andy instead played a junkman who builds a rocket out of scraps and travels to the moon on the TV show *Salvage 1*. (In one episode he and his crew meet an alien from Andromeda who looks exactly like Andy.) Late in Andy's career, when he was hungry for substantial work, the auteur Joan Micklin Silver asked him to perform in a screen adaptation of the Paul Osborn play *Mornings at Seven*. The project was never made.

There were also two failed marriages, with the first divorce delivering strained relationships with his children. His oldest child, a boy named Andy Jr., called Sam, born not long after the release of *A Face in the Crowd*, died tragically in 1996, of an overdose of pills and complications related to alcoholism, before his fortieth birthday. Sam had been in and out of trouble since he was fifteen, when he was picked up by the Los Angeles police for selling pot; once the cops found out who he was, they brought him home to Toluca Lake rather than arrest him.

Andy loved his children and did his best, but he didn't know what to do with Sam after he began drinking and smoking and doing drugs. Sam was a violent drinker and did time in jail for physically abusing his second wife. After the trial, Andy paid Sam's close friend Mickey $5,000 a month to keep Sam from getting in more trouble and to keep him clear of the tabloids. Sam didn't mind the attention, but Andy did not like sharing the spotlight, especially with those kinds of stories. When Andy and Barbara divorced in 1972, she got roughly half of everything, which was better than the $100-a-week household allowance Dick Linke had insisted on when she and Andy were married and Andy was earning millions. And when Barbara died in 1980 at the age of fifty-three, Sam and Dixie, barely in their twenties, each inherited half of Barbara's estate, which included so much of what Andy's career had built and Dick Linke's suggested investments. They owned real estate holdings, including office buildings and apartment complexes all over the San Fernando Valley and elsewhere. Andy had provided. Barbara and Andy both had. Still, Andy felt as if he'd failed Sam.

38.

I imagine Andy Griffith didn't consider many of his failures radically different from his successes. Objectively, the failures outweighed the successes, but his successes were complete and profound. The lasting impact of Andy's first film role, starring in Elia Kazan's *A Face in the Crowd*, is still felt. The ripples on the water are still moving. Elvis Costello is mounting a Broadway musical stage adaptation, intended to debut in the near future. He's been performing songs from the show in recent concerts. Screen directors as varied as Steven Spielberg, Peyton Reed, and Spike Lee list *A Face in the Crowd* as one of their favorite films. Reed told the *Telegraph* in 2003, "It might not be his best film, but for me it's his most fascinating." Spike Lee's great film *Bamboozled* (2000) was directly inspired by *A Face in the Crowd*, and Lee shared with PBS that *A Face in the Crowd* was one of three films everyone should see. Steven Spielberg delivered an introduction to the film and underscored its importance at a screening of it in 2017 at Hollywood's Egyptian Theatre as part of the American Cinematheque's program. The director said of *A Face in the Crowd*, "In my opinion, [it is] nothing short of a masterpiece." And many in the industry recall that Andy's portrayal of Lonesome Rhodes is one of the great performances of the century. *Matlock* ran for nine seasons and pleased millions and is still in syndication. But *The Andy Griffith Show* is unique in the pantheon of great television comedies. Many lists include it in the top ten best sitcoms of all time. For many, it's number one. It's transcendent. *The Andy Griffith Show* has been on TV for over sixty years, and there are people, so many people, who've radically altered the course of their lives because of this old comedy broadcast, including me.

39.

On my way to Mount Airy, North Carolina, for the third time, to research this book, I detoured through Charlottesville, Virginia, following a story that didn't pan out. This was before the violence there, when white supremacists killed a young woman. I was there to speak with someone about southern comedy, and my source agreed to meet with me at a bar downtown but then never showed. The next morning, waking alone in the gloom of the cheapest hotel I could find on the Priceline app and checking my almost empty bank account, I turned on the news and tried to gather my notes, and wits, and see what work plan I could muster. On the hotel TV was breaking news that a fighter jet from Massachusetts had crashed that morning in the Virginia mountains. I checked the map, saw that the area was about an hour away, and thought, what the hell, maybe I can report the search and rescue effort as it's happening for a news outlet like the *Boston Globe*, which might lead to more work and my kids won't see me as a failure. I packed up my few things, which was a smelly backpack and a dopp kit; pointed my ancient, beaten-up dad wagon west; and checked my cracked old phone for directions. I was the first to pull in the gravel parking lot at the news staging area, which was the community's volunteer fire department.

Two men sat in the shade of a rusty corrugated metal roof held aloft by solid timber posts and a milled lumber frame. A. D. Shinaberry and Nelson Bartley nodded as I approached. They rested at one of the four rough picnic tables spaced in a row on the shelter's poured concrete floor, their bodies leaning against the table in a familiar posture. My uncle Jack Simmons sat that way after a summer day painting the shutters, bending wrought iron, any physical work. Jack moved in with us after his last tour of Vietnam, not long after my dad was killed. I witnessed Jack rest in the shade of the garage just as these men sat—as if life is long and there is much more to do, and I'll damn well do it, but not right this damn minute.

"There were two booms," Mr. Shinaberry said, a forty-eight-year veteran of the Deerfield, Virginia, volunteer fire and rescue. (Mr. Bartley had recently celebrated his fiftieth year of service.) The fire station was a squat brick building that served the fewer than 200 souls that lived in this remote valley situated in the shadow of the Shenandoah Mountains, as well as the hikers and campers who ventured inside the valley's span of George Washington National Forest—over 1 million densely wooded and mountainous acres of federal land across two states. The national forest dominates the region; the great Shenandoah National Park, with its Civil War breastworks, rugged campsites, and ample wildlife, is entirely inside its borders.

"Each boom shook the ground. About ten seconds apart." Mr. Shinaberry stood and pointed toward Great North Mountain. "That's where the smoke was, like a mushroom cloud, just to that side of those trees, on the flat side."

A news crew from Roanoke arrived. A few minutes later the AP reporter from Richmond pulled his Subaru alongside the other vehicles in the meadow behind the rescue station. There were narrow wooden bleachers in the field, used for ball games and livestock shows. The reporter quickly set up his black laptop at the table behind us, with a peripheral Internet device and a coiled antenna to boost the signal, and began typing, listening to me interview the two gentlemen. A young camera operator with tattoos snaking across his forearm eyed the reporter's small antenna. "I have to get one of those." No one had a cell phone signal. We were inside what is known as a National Quiet Zone.

Mr. Shinaberry said, "You know Verizon says, 'Can you hear me now?' You can't hear me now here." I immediately gave up on the idea of reporting this live to a news outlet— for its Twitter feed or website or as a stringer for another reporter. Besides, I couldn't pitch anyone from the scene over text or email or even make a call.

Three helicopters were in the air, searching. An unconfirmed report circulated that the pilot ejected—the rescue contingent looked for signs of a parachute in the thick forest canopy. It was a warm late-summer day. It was painfully beautiful there. Winding narrow roads through dense woods opened up to a succession of pristine farms, each with a half dozen Black Angus cattle lazing in the shade of a white oak, baled hay dotted across a green expanse bordered by a burbling stream, a pond stocked with trout. It would make you weep. There was life everywhere: bobcats in the woods, black bears.

"We saw your Massachusetts plates when you came in. We wondered about that. Did you know the pilot was flying out of Massachusetts?"

"Yes, I heard that before I came."

Mr. Shinaberry turned. "There's another one." A fourth helicopter joined the search. Another news crew arrived. More satellite trucks. News Channel 7. News Channel 10. A crew set up an array of black tripods on the other end of the shadowed picnic shelter.

"Did you say your wife's family was from around Charlottesville?" Mr. Shinaberry asked me.

"No."

I didn't offer that I was no longer married, that it was raw, that I was without a home, and that my anxiety only ceased in the cab of my car, a family wagon, a vestige from an earlier life. I had said as much to wincing cashiers, baristas, bank tellers, that I was unmoored, that in the back of my car were all my clothes and most of my belongings, the back seat littered with my children's toys and Disney-themed backpacks, a canvas tote bag filled with beach gear, still sandy—buckets, shovels, face masks, and snorkels, a pink one and a blue one—the beach towels damp and moldering. I told them I was traveling the country working on a book about Andy Griffith, which was true.

"My grandmother's family is from Patrick County, Virginia. Down by the North Carolina line. My aunts and uncles live there still."

Mr. Shinaberry nodded and watched a helicopter approach, the blade's rotation impossibly slow. "Bootlegger country."

"That's true," I said and then turned back to the reason we were there. "Are there a lot of military flights over these mountains?"

"Military planes used to fly daily. Now, not so much. They'd fly below radar, training."

"Did that bother anybody?" the AP reporter asked.

"It used to bother your turkeys," Mr. Bartley said.

"How many turkeys do you have, Mr. Shinaberry?"

"Fifty thousand. I grew your Thanksgiving turkey."

Another news crew arrived. Mr. Bartley stood. "That's my cue to leave. I've no interest in being on television."

A press conference was scheduled for later in the day. Helicopters landed and dropped rescuers off; more rescuers boarded, and the helicopters took off again. Black SUVs arrived, as did several identical white sedans with yellow sirens, agents racing to assist from a nearby training exercise. In the end, nine aircraft circled above the Shenandoah and the community of Deerfield, Virginia. In total, thirty federal and state agencies helped in the search for the missing pilot, over a hundred people, including volunteers. The rescuers were fed by still more volunteers. They did not know the pilot's name, only that earlier in the day a Massachusetts Air National Guard pilot flying to New Orleans for a routine systems upgrade had reported an in-flight emergency and that shortly after, his F-15 had crashed. The next day, Thursday, when the still smoldering debris field could be examined, it was determined the pilot—Lt. Col. Morris Fontenot Jr., a decorated veteran, a husband, and a father—remained with his plane.

Before that happened, on Wednesday, as the volunteers, officials, and media gathered at Deerfield Fire and Rescue, I turned off the main road and entered the forest, winding up a crushed stone and dirt lane that ambled up the mountain, slowing to a crawl where flooding had exposed sharp rocks I feared would pop the car's bald tires and strand me. Every so often I looked at the No Service status on my phone out of dumb habit. I inched along, scanning the lush woods, looking for anything at all. This story would end far better with a parachute—stitched together to save us from falling, some bright, man-made color among the wilderness. I wanted to be of use. To be helpful. Maybe my kids would see.

A black bear ran across the dirt road about fifty yards ahead of me, its body like a thick, broad-shouldered man walking on all fours. A man in a bear suit. He moved at a steady clip with nothing that radiated fear, then was lost.

The trail climbed until I came to two forks, leading still higher, blocked by wooden barricades. I turned the car around and drove back down.

40.

On a warm September evening in 2010, after dinner, bubble baths, teeth brushing, diaper changing, pajama dressing, and storytelling, I helped wrangle my two young children to bed and kissed them both good night. It was the first and only time I had ever been away from them. I set out on a long journey from my home in New York City to a place I'd never been, an island in South Carolina, to attend the funeral of a man I didn't know.

Stopping only a few hours later for the night in Princeton, New Jersey, I met up with my traveling companion, my older sister—a woman a few years my senior, whom I'd had dinner and drinks with for the first time in the previous year. Early the next morning, she said so long to her three daughters and her grumbling, recently ex-husband and hopped in the passenger seat of my car to direct me to Charlotte, North Carolina, where we'd stay the night with her younger sister, whom I'd never before met. We traveled in a caravan the next day for Hilton Head.

The funeral was our father's. In Hilton Head, we'd meet another sister, the middle child, tall like me, and the leader of the group. She spoke at the service. I also met two younger brothers, men now, but both over ten years my junior. My sisters had not seen them since they were toddlers. I met my brothers for the first time in their modest hotel room an hour before the funeral. I changed into my only suit in their bathroom. I learned later that the middle sister had paid for their room, as they'd both been laid off as a result of the financial collapse. I dumped the plastic wrap and the cheap wire hangers from my neighborhood dry cleaner in their tiny hotel wastebasket. The refuse overwhelmed the little receptacle; I was embarrassed at the sight of it as I wrestled with the overly small knot of my ill-chosen necktie.

41.

My kids and I devoured our Shake Shack burgers and fries at the metal tables in Madison Square Park. I'd happily waited in the long line while they played under a London plane tree a few feet away. We lingered afterward in the playground and looked at the just-installed summer art—Orly Genger's giant colored rope sculptures. My kids loved the sculptures, made a game of which color was their favorite, wanted to trace their hands along the weaves. Then, exhausted, full, it was time to go home, and rather than take the M14 bus on Fourteenth Street, we walked. I carried my four-year-old daughter on my shoulders, her hands on my ears and in my hair, my left hand raised and keeping her steady, and I gripped my eight-year-old son's hand with my right. I told my daughter that on my shoulders she was the tallest kid in Manhattan, just like her brother had been when he was her age. We walked down Broadway past Union Square. I stood huge, smiling and laughing with my kids and strangers alike. We turned on Twelfth and walked east toward their old elementary school, then down Second Avenue, across Houston to Allen, down to Grand, and then east toward home. My back was strained and I was drenched, and my daughter was perfectly capable of walking, but I didn't care. I'd been in the neighborhood for over fifteen years, the length of my marriage, and it was the only home my children knew. There were more stops along the way, I'm sure: the Pickle Guys, Kossar's, Doughnut Plant. I wanted them to enjoy their neighborhood a little longer, as much as possible, as I knew it was ending. Their mother had left. She wasn't coming back. I didn't know it for sure, as I was left in the dark about everything, but I knew it. Certain friends pulled me aside and said they knew I was a good father, that I took care of the kids, but don't fight. Move to Boston. I carried my daughter and held my son's hand and walked all the way home because I wanted all of New York City to see how much I loved them, how proud I was of them, and that I was theirs and they were mine.

42.

When Andy Griffith died, I cried. I was a grown man with two young children in school, working at my low-level editorial job in an office at the bottom tip of Manhattan, on a high floor in an old building overlooking New York Harbor. On a clear day I could see the long Verrazano Bridge stretching from Staten Island into Brooklyn, its engineers and architects accounting for the curve of the earth when it was built. The giant orange Staten Island Ferry slowly docked and then took off again at the base of the East River as I stared at my computer display, my eyes welling. I was upset that this man, whom I had never once met or seen in person or spoken to, had died. This man I didn't know was like a father to me.

There's a YouTube video of the 911 call when Andy Griffith died. A video of a phone call. Let that sink in for a moment. The YouTube video is a dark screen with transcribed audio. The 911 dispatcher speaks calmly; the voice on the other end is that of a caretaker, an employee, a friend. The young man explains that that they found Andy on the ground. He had fallen out of his chair and was unresponsive.

43.

In a small but growing community in Effingham County, Georgia, in the county seat of Springfield, population not that many but more than before, as it pitches and changes under the boom and sway of nearby Savannah, a man has died. He died in his car, a black 2009 Nissan Altima, in traffic, on a highway, with people passing in their vehicles going quickly from one place to another, slowing down to peer at the smoking aftermath, the blue and red lights bouncing against the asphalt embankment and the bent gray metal guardrail. The ambulance arrived and raced off, the traffic between city and country sped up again, the broken glass and refuse was swept away. It was an accident.

The man who died was a pastor and Sunday school teacher at a Baptist church in Effingham County. He often used clips and quotes from *The Andy Griffith Show* in his lessons and sermons, especially when teaching the kids. It was his favorite show.

Outside the funeral, in front of the church, a replica Mayberry squad car was on display. The local newspaper wrote about the event and photoshopped Don Knotts as Barney Fife inside the driver's seat, waiting outside the church.

A quote from Andy Griffith was printed on the program for the funeral. It was taken from an article Andy wrote to promote his second gospel album, but in the funeral program it was attributed to his character on *The Andy Griffith Show*, Andy Taylor.

Inside, during the funeral service, on a giant screen, a clip from *The Andy Griffith Show* played.

44.

The sky was severe blue—clear and expansive. A large American flag flapped with the breeze alongside colored streamers and red, white, and blue balloons tethered to the town center's telephone poles and street signs. The little town square was bustling with people. The familiar smell of charred burgers and barbecue smoke from slow-roasted pork shoulder filled the air, along with hot dogs, chili, fried dough, and cornbread—the sounds and wafting odors of food vendors dominated the side parking lots of downtown buildings dedicated to the commerce involved with a festival.

On stage, a squat man in a costume of black vest, torn blue work pants, and black boots, with another ill-fitting costume of shiny gold-sequined lamé lazily draped in a layer over his black vest, warbled Elvis Presley's "Love Me Tender." The man, a part-time actor from Mount Olive, North Carolina, Phil Fox, was playing a recurring character from *The Andy Griffith Show*, Ernest T. Bass, playing an Elvis impersonator. The effect was startling and hilarious. A handful of aging adults and adolescents took in the sight as if it were completely normal.

The comedic actor Howard Morris, who actually played the part of Ernest T. Bass on *The Andy Griffith Show*, appeared on only a handful of episodes across eight seasons but had a long career. He had been a featured performer on Sid Caesar's famed *Your Show of Shows* in the early 1950s, where so many comedy greats got their foothold, including Carl Reiner, Mel Brooks, Neil Simon, and

Imogene Coca. Howard Morris was a respected director and classically trained actor, with numerous credits, yet where he rests for eternity at Hillside Memorial Park and Mortuary, in Culver City, California, the brass plaque above his name and years on earth reads, "It's me, it's me, it's Ernest T."

45.

In Mount Airy, North Carolina, at the Mayberry Days festival, an Elvis impersonator locked his keys in his burgundy Toyota Camry and attempted to gain entry by using a metal coat hanger slipped through the driver's-side window.

46.

In the spring of 1968, when he was a freshman at New York University, Gary Frank attended a screening of *A Face in the Crowd.* He fell in love with the film, and later, at his favorite collectibles shop on the Upper West Side of Manhattan, he found a giant poster used to advertise the movie when it was released in 1957. He framed the poster and hung it on the wall in his room at his childhood home in Queens. A few years later, Elia Kazan was screening *A Face in the Crowd* at Lincoln Center in New York City. Less than twenty years after its release, the film was heralded a masterpiece. Gary removed the poster from the frame, rolled it up, caught the train to the city, attended the screening, and waited patiently in the lobby, after the Q&A, for Elia Kazan to appear. Gary approached casually and asked the great director to sign his poster. Kazan did so graciously. Gary thanked him and headed home. It was his first autograph. Over the years, many more times, he took the poster out of its frame and rolled it up and traveled to wherever a maker of the film was appearing or speaking. He met Walter Matthau and Patricia Neal at the Ninety-Second Street Y and Lee Remick at an event at the Film Forum. One by one, Gary Frank asked them to sign his poster. He flew to Los Angeles, the poster riding in the plane's overhead compartment, and met Budd Schulberg at the Los Angeles County Museum of Art. Finally, he got Andy Griffith to sign, just outside the *Today Show* in 1996.

47.

At a Mayberry Days event in 2015, in Mount Airy, North Carolina, the actor Clint Howard spoke to the audience in attendance:

> What it reminds me, is, first of all, how good the show was, because people connected with it. I can tell, you guys, this is not a *Star Trek* convention, or this isn't a horror convention, and they don't do this for the *Beverly Hillbillies*. There was something special about it . . . and I can tell when you guys come up to me, I can see by the look in your eye what the show meant. And that reminds me it's something to really be proud of. And I am. I'm proud for my brother, and my dad, and just everybody. This is something special. This is not pabulum. It's not heavy-handed. It's just well constructed, not wholesome—it's honest entertainment.

48.

Late one hot evening in the summer of 2010, I drove east-ward in a caravan of three vehicles—the types of cars young families own, two minivans followed by my Subaru wagon—along a dead-straight empty stretch of Fording Island Road, my back to the island of Hilton Head, South Carolina. It was my first and only visit to the place, which lasted approximately nine hours. I ventured there to attend my biological father's funeral—a complicated man I never once met or spoke to or heard anything from. I learned more of him in that afternoon than I'd accumulated in almost thirty years of searching out information about him. I met my siblings for the first time, though we'd known about each other, that we existed, for most of our lives.

All four of my car windows were down; the air was per-fumed and fragrant with pinesap and salt. I drove alone, the car stereo playing Built to Spill's *Perfect from Now On.* The album has instrumental crescendos, jangling guitar, rolling drums—it builds and builds, as if climbing a high moun-tain in order to shout something important off it, and that is what happened: I began shouting. The dim lights of my newly met sister's Honda were a quarter-mile ahead; our eldest sister sat beside her in the passenger seat. The mid-dle sister and her family led the way in a Toyota Sienna. We were driving 100 miles north to her home in Charleston, swift through the inky night.

The last song on Built to Spill's album, a sprawling nine-minute number called "Untrustable Part 2," reaches for a kind of epiphany, its driving drum and bass and jingle-jangle guitar moving along with a smattering of percussion, including a high hat and what sounds like a tambourine. Around the six-minute mark the song can no longer sustain itself—something breaks, seemingly goes backward in time, and then builds again to its close at 8:54. Knowing this simple math, I can safely claim I screamed at the top of my lungs for over three minutes as I followed my new family. It was more than screaming—I've never made noises like this before or since. Screaming or yelling is not an accurate description. It was a guttural sound, from somewhere buried within my large frame, primal. Not quite a howl, but there was longing in it, and anger and rage, loss, frustration—almost as if I was heaving some sickness out of my body, but it wasn't merely physical (nothing is ever merely physical). My eyes were wet and I must have been sobbing, but I don't recall the act of crying, only the strange sounds I made as the music played and I followed the two cars along the dark highway. We were our absent father's children fleeing the town our father fled to in 1975. In 2010, I was forty-one, married with two small children. This dead man, my biological father, was seventy-six; only a year before he had been discovered late one night wandering around the neighbor's yard and then was diagnosed with Alzheimer's. He eventually stopped communicating, and then eating, until he wasted to almost nothing, and ceased to exist.

49.

I have three fathers. One who married my mother when they both were teenagers and who died when I was five; another, my natural father, who worked with my mom and dad, supplied half my DNA, and never, in fact, wanted to meet me; and Andy Griffith, a television surrogate, who arrived every day in the den of our house on WFMY Channel 2.

50.

I spoke with the comedy writer Emily Spivey about her career and pitched a story to an editor about her show *Up All Night*, which starred Christina Applegate, Will Arnett, and Maya Rudolph. The series was a single-camera sitcom, like *The Andy Griffith Show*, and produced by Lorne Michaels, whom Spivey had worked with for many years at *Saturday Night Live*. After two seasons, Lorne Michaels decided for its third season to change the format from a one-camera show—which is shot like a movie and its sets look like real homes, with natural light and lots of outdoor location scenes, again, like *The Andy Griffith Show* or *Parks and Recreation*—to a three-camera sitcom, onstage in front of an audience, like *Married with Children*. The lead actors walked, then Spivey walked, and the show was canceled. She didn't want to speak with me about it. Maybe a year later, when I was alone in Massachusetts and out of work, I designed some coffee mugs to sell online, hoping maybe I could make some money to buy holiday gifts for my kids. My daughter had asked for an American Girl doll, which cost as much as a used car. The mugs read, "How would Lubitsch do it?" I thought maybe the mugs would make a nice crew gift, so I DM'd people I knew in the entertainment industry to tell them about my stupid mugs, and then Emily Spivey blocked me on Twitter. I don't blame her. What an asshole I was, selling coffee mugs. Below are excerpts from an interview I conducted with Spivey over email—before she blocked me on Twitter—to illustrate Andy Griffith's legacy in modern comedy. Spivey wrote:

My second job was as a writer on the show *King of the Hill*. I'm convinced I got the job because in my interview with Greg Daniels, we bonded over our mutual love for *The Andy Griffith Show*. He had a framed map of Mayberry on his wall. Greg told me that he loved the humor of *The Andy Griffith Show* but he also loved it because it was a very humane show. The characters really cared for each other in a real and touching way. Greg (and Mike Schur) still carry out that Andy Griffith/Andy Taylor tradition on *Parks and Recreation*, which I think is a modern *Andy Griffith Show*. Pawnee is totally Mayberry. I had the pleasure of working on that show [*Parks and Recreation*] as well. All the humor and stories come out of the love and compassion the characters have for each other.

I think growing up in North Carolina offers a unique experience, especially at the time I was coming along. This was before the Internet and a million DirecTV channels. As a result, you really had to search for the things and people that interested you. It helped to cultivate a super specific point of view. Having had the most awkward, fugly middle school years ever, I found relief in finding a group of like-minded comedy nerds. . . . Comedy was like our church. But the amazing thing about growing up in the South and North Carolina is that you are also going to ACTUAL church, which offers up a whole host of crazy, funny, contradictory situations and characters. Those situations and folks inform my comedy POV until this very day.

The amount of college campuses also afforded NC kids the best of both worlds. Even if you grew up in a little mill town, as I did, you were just a hop skip and a jump from Greensboro or Chapel Hill, towns that had amazing book stores, museums, music clubs, record stores. So you got the best of both worlds. It's different than being born and raised in a big city where you never experience the beauty and hilarity of the small town perspective. Also, at the time at least, I was afforded a wonderful public school education, including Governor's School, a summer program, which influenced my writing, way of thinking and creativity in a profoundly positive way.

I loved listening to my nutty, older southern relatives, my father in particular, who all were endlessly funny, whether they meant to be or not. My Dad is hilarious. Humor and being funny was valued in my house. My Dad is an OG comedy nerd.

After graduating from UNCG [the University of North Carolina–Greensboro], I went to LA to go to graduate school at Loyola Marymount. It was like moving into a Dr. Seuss book, everything looked twisted and weird and sprawling and I was homesick for green and seasons. People commented on my NC accent a lot, which surprised me. I worked to tamp it down. But as I got older, I began to embrace it again and landed my first job [*Mad TV*] by auditioning with quite a few southern characters and sketches.

Luckily, I found a gently used American Girl doll on Craigslist from a nice family in Framingham, Massachusetts. They kindly included extra clothes, and handmade shoes, as the original shoes, like so many things, were lost.

51.

In the summer of 2002, I was crouched on the grooved metal floor of a relatively clean white Chevy cargo van that was ferrying the band Guided by Voices from Brooklyn to Manhattan. The band was exiting a massive Matador Records–sponsored party thrown in GBV's honor at the warehouse-sized event space inside the Brooklyn Brewery and headed to the music venue Irving Plaza, where the group was ushering in its latest album, *Universal Truths and Cycles*. The ride lasted maybe twenty minutes. For the entirety of the trip, Robert Pollard—Guided by Voices' celebrated front man and prolific songwriter—spoke only of Andy Griffith. As his bandmates casually drank cans of beer, laughed, and made small talk, Robert Pollard quoted lines from *The Andy Griffith Show*. Speaking out of the corner of his mouth, eyes gleeful, Pollard said, "Andy looks up at Aunt Bee, 'I ate four bowls—if that ain't a tribute to white beans, I don't know what is.'" I traced my finger along the rutted floor and watched the glory of the Manhattan skyline at dusk as we inched across the Williamsburg Bridge, and Pollard repeated a bit louder, "Andy looked up at Aunt Bee, 'Well, I ate four bowls—if that ain't a tribute to white beans, I don't know what is.'" Pollard giggled, sipped his Budweiser. He was ignoring most everyone in the van. It was unclear whether he was speaking to anyone in particular. Pollard said again, quieter, laughing as he spoke, "'If that ain't a tribute to white beans, I don't know what is.'"

I heard my name.

"Evan is the biggest Andy Griffith fan in the world."

"Who's Evan?" Pollard asked.

"He's sitting on the floor right there."

I looked up with a nervous smile and locked eyes with Robert Pollard.

"You love Andy Griffith?" Pollard asked.

"Yes."

"So do I."

52.

The recent and endless political struggles in North Carolina put me in mind of a buried bit of North Carolina history. When tugged out from under the sediment that's been shoveled atop it over 140 years it still shines, and its brightness burns away at least some of the hazy mythology that floats over the culture. Many people raised there, like Andy Griffith, inherit this myth, either as ugly luggage to carry around and fret over, or to lift above their heads like a banner. Having left North Carolina in 1995 in my mid-twenties—driving a rusted '82 Chevette up the Eastern Seaboard with stenciled black stars spray-painted across the car's roof, its interior packed to the seams with all my worldly possessions—I was eager to see what the larger world offered. I soon discovered that living anywhere else immediately provided the sudden knowledge that the place I'd come from, the home I'd left, this North Carolina, the Tar Heel State, is entirely unique and that I was inextricably shaped by its rich and complicated blend of culture—which is fundamentally, wildly at odds with itself.

During the Civil War, a Union man from just across the border in east Tennessee named George Washington Kirk gathered around him a force of sympathetic southerners to fight, sabotage, and destroy the work of the secessionists—well behind Confederate lines. In surviving photographs, Kirk appears handsome, fearless. In one image he sits confidently—square-jawed, head slightly cocked, a look of daring in his eyes—beside his attractive wife, Louisa, dark, thin, and elegant. The young man and woman look a bit like they could be representatives of the current crop of North Carolina's numerous indie-rock stars, maybe the Avett Brothers, or a band signed with world-famous Merge Records, the home label of Arcade Fire and Lambchop.

Kirk's orders were to destroy Confederate provisions and rain havoc and hell on rebel supporters, recruiting new Union soldiers along the way from the steady stream of Confederate deserters and North Carolina mountain boys who were ready to join their older brothers already fighting for the Union in Kentucky and Tennessee. Kirk's men were almost all from western North Carolina, stretching from the lush rolling hills of the Piedmont, with its concentration of red clay and abolitionist Quakers, to the rugged and beautiful land on either side of what is now the rhododendron-dappled Blue Ridge Parkway, including Surry County, the childhood home of Andy Griffith.

G. W. Kirk and his soldiers were guerrilla warriors yet had official orders from a commanding general of the Army of the Ohio. Their designation was the Third North Carolina Mounted Division, although mounts weren't provided. They often moved on foot to avoid detection, and after a task was achieved they made their way back on stolen or captured horses. These assignments were in harmony with William Tecumseh Sherman's grand scheme of denying the enemy supply and comfort. In fact, General Sherman sent his hearty congratulations to Colonel Kirk after daring and successful attacks on Camp Vance and a supply depot at Morganton, North Carolina.

Camp Vance, a Confederate training camp, was reduced to ash, save for its hospital, and Kirk destroyed a cache of weapons in Morganton along with tons of military supplies, 250 bushels of corn, and a train. When he withdrew to Union-held Knoxville, seemingly moving through the western North Carolina counties with ease, Kirk delivered forty recruits, forty horses and mules, and 132 prisoners of war.

Since the majority of the recorded history of this unit was written from a pro-Confederate point of view, Kirk is often remembered as a blood-lusting partisan, a looter, and a thief. (He appears in one municipal mural wearing a jangling belt of silverware.) Yet Kirk was almost entirely successful at his military tasks, exercising brutal efficiency. Whatever his temper, he was good at his job, if not exceptional. According to William Trotter's *Bushwhackers*, a history that Charles Frazier lists as a source for his popular Civil War fiction, *Cold Mountain*, "If Kirk needed a large force, he sent out word and the men came in; and if he needed a small, stealthy reconnaissance force, he knew just who to pick for that kind of mission, too." Kirk's raiders suffered few losses, traveled with quickness and ease (they were, after all, locals), and with the help of a large underground resistance called Heroes of America, or Red Strings, always made their way back to Federal lines.

The name Red Strings came about because these Union supporters wore a red string in their lapel to indicate their secret allegiance. Their true numbers are unknown but estimated at over 10,000. Many had decades-long practice at subterfuge, providing safe harbor to the men, women, and children who escaped slavery.

According to the testimony of William Hickman, who as a teen volunteered when two of Kirk's recruiting officers came to his home village of Mount Airy, North Carolina, it was harrowing business making their way northwest—one of the officers was killed, and many recruits fled, but still, Hickman also believed some of the home guard were shooting into the air rather than directly at them. He explained to his daughter at the end of his years, "We had Union men all through the settlement, and every one of us knew our neighbor's convictions. The Union recruiters had a regular route they traveled once a month or more. This route we called an underground railway."

The recruiter who lived through this particular episode was my ancestor Meshack Jessup, whose home and hearth was only a few miles away. Meshack Jessup's daughter married a Simmons, whose uncle was Andy Griffith's great-great-great-grandfather. This Simmons daughter married a Taylor. Both families were old Quaker families that settled in Westfield, which is east of Mount Airy, toward Winston-Salem, and named Westfield because in the colonial era it was settled by Quakers from the New Garden Friends meetings in Guilford County. Andy and I are third cousins. Most of these families, including mine and Andy's, married outside their religion and were kicked out of the Quaker church and became Methodist or Baptist, so they were no longer were pacifists and could serve in the army when the conscription officers came and rounded people up.

Andy's direct Simmons ancestor (who was the brother of my direct Simmons ancestor) is buried in an unmarked grave in the Civil War section of Hollywood

Cemetery in downtown Richmond, Virginia, not too far from the giant stone pyramid that the Daughters of the Confederacy put up, back in the heyday of monuments to white supremacy. A pyramid! Amos Simmons died of gangrene in 1863. My children, my sister Logan, one of her sons, and I found the grave on a hot day in August, and then I treated everyone to sandwiches at Jersey Mike's sub shop across the street.

Regardless of how much assistance and safe passage Colonel Kirk had, he often ambitiously attempted to extend his orders. Asked to destroy the Yadkin River bridge, he hatched a scheme to also steal a locomotive seventy-five miles behind enemy lines, where the railroad began in Morganton, and speed the train and his men another eighty miles into the interior—almost to the center of North Carolina, to the infamous Salisbury prison, the state's only prisoner-of-war camp, which existed on sixteen acres, its main building an abandoned tin-roofed cotton factory. By 1865 the prison's population outnumbered the 2,000 souls who lived in the town of Salisbury by a factor of five, with likely a rival number buried in the eighteen football-field-length trenches that served as mass graves. (It's now a national cemetery.) Kirk's plan was to liberate the fortified prison, fill the train with freed soldiers, and zoom back along the tracks.

I don't know if Meshack Jessup was among Kirk's men on the Morganton mission. I know very little of his life. Meshack deserted the Confederate army at Drewry's Bluff, Virginia, in 1862 and by 1864 was ferrying young Union recruits through the mountains to muster out in Tennessee. A spy. If caught, he'd have been executed.

It's telling we don't know the reach or history of the Order of Heroes of America. Their exploits were mostly buried and forgotten—their numbers, motives, and true actions all unknown. The unified Lost Cause narrative that arose decades after the war didn't allow room for a competing history.

After the devastation and ruin that marked the end of the Civil War, during Reconstruction, in 1870, African Americans in North Carolina were terrorized by the Ku Klux Klan and denied the right to vote—a right that had been adopted and guaranteed by the state's newly drafted constitution of 1868, largely spearheaded by an interesting and complicated longtime North Carolina political figure named Thomas Settle.

There were numerous beatings, whippings, and degradations. A white schoolteacher, Alonzo Corliss, who taught Black children the ABCs had his head shaved and tarred. Then the Klan murdered two men: John Stephens, a Republican state senator, was knifed in the basement of the Caswell County Courthouse; and Wyatt Outlaw, an African American night police officer of the town of Graham, was lynched in Alamance County. (You may recognize Alamance if you've driven the interstate highways of North Carolina, as it's known now for its outlet malls.) Governor William Woods Holden, a prominent newspaper editor turned politician, declared martial law and called George Washington Kirk back into the fray to put down the insurrection. Kirk gathered 300 volunteers from western North Carolina, rode into town, and immediately commenced shit-kicking, arresting around fifty Klansmen, who also were prominent businessmen, attorneys, and civic leaders, including the local sheriff. Thomas Settle, acting as a court justice, oversaw their arrest. A federal judge eventually released the Klan members—none were tried.

There was a backlash to the mass arrests. The Conservative-held North Carolina legislature led a successful revolt against Holden, resulting in the first impeachment and removal of a state governor in America's history. Legislators also wrangled the arrest of G. W. Kirk, but he was secretly released and made his way back to Tennessee, perhaps with one hand on his revolver. George was welcomed home by Louisa, son John, and his youngest, five-year-old William Tecumseh Kirk. The months-long police action became known as the Kirk-Holden War.

Over the next few years, the North Carolina legislature took steps to reshape the government to ensure that Conservatives remained in power, challenged only by the Progressive Thomas Settle in the governor's race of 1876, a vote that largely decided how North Carolina imagines itself.

After the suppression of Reconstruction and reform, North Carolinians, for fear of retribution, kept secret that they had once called themselves Heroes of America and worn a red thread on their lapels. Conservatives gained full power in the governor's election of 1876, after adding several constitutional amendments in 1875, including a ban on mixed-race marriage, which they thought would be eternal. Until *Loving v. Virginia* in 1967 overturned bans on mixed-race marriages nationwide, the constitution of North Carolina still retained its 1875 language, stating such marriages "are forever prohibited."

I can only guess at my ancestor Meshack Jessup's beliefs. He was from a branch of an old Quaker family who'd married outside the religion; his grandfather took his wife and ten of their eleven children to Indiana in the 1830s, all save Meshack's dad, Eli. During the time Meshack was in George Washington Kirk's group of raiders, he had a toddler at home in Surry County named Ruth, who grew up to marry a tall, broad-shouldered Surry County man, William Washington Simmons. Ruth and Will named their firstborn Thomas Settle Simmons, after Thomas Settle.

Dr. Jeffrey Crow, in his 1996 essay "Thomas Settle Jr., Reconstruction, and the Memory of the Civil War," published in the *Journal of Southern History*, argues that during the historic moment of the election of 1876, the pervasive idea of the southern Lost Cause and its "noble fallen" hadn't taken hold; that romantic notion was adopted decades later. It was a comfortable story for the Conservative leadership, to ignore that protecting the economic interests of a minority of wealthy planters had wrought pain, death, poverty, and scorched earth for North Carolina. The state had the most contention and internal strife of the Confederate states before and throughout the Civil War and also suffered the greatest losses. With so many dead in such a short time, it's impossible not to create a mythology to adorn the still fresh graves. This was easier than to look back to the radical moment at the close of the war, a time of reconsideration, reinvention, which is where Settle's 1876 debate rhetoric landed in the imagination.

Thomas Settle, of course, lost, by 14,000 votes. He won 47 percent of the vote. The constitutional amendments

were solidified. After the election, one of Settle's supporters asked, "What do the poor and humble mean by voting
away their liberties?"

In the late 1970s and 1980s, after the election of Senator Jesse Helms and his dominance of national politics
(Helms had started his career as a pro-segregationist
radio disc jockey and, among much else, was anti–civil
rights and anti–gay rights and at least in conversation
said he supported the death penalty for homosexuality),
some who had Andy Griffith's ear tried to convince him
to run for public office. He was a good friend with many
leaders. He'd met Governor Luther Hodges in the 1950s,
backstage when Andy was on Broadway, performing in
No Time for Sergeants; Hodges later would declare "Andy
Griffith Day" statewide in 1957. Andy become friends and
business partners with Terry Sanford. Maybe he could
do some good if he ran against Jesse. But Andy had also
been a hard drinker and womanizer until at least the mid-
1970s, had hosted all-night parties at his estate, and had
performed at dozens of casinos and nightclubs, and his
agents' and managers' connections to underworld crime
figures were suspicious at best. Yet Andy had somehow avoided coverage by the tabloids and had no public
scandals.

In 1977, among his small stable of clients, Dick Linke
managed Andy Griffith, Frankie Avalon, and a ventril-
oquist named Jay Johnson, who was made famous by
the show *Soap*, which aired later that year. Dick Linke
instructed these entertainers to perform a free show at the
ballroom of a motor lodge in Wilkes-Barre, Pennsylvania,
for the annual dinner sponsored by the Italian American

Civil Rights League, celebrating the birthday of one of its leaders, Russell Bufalino. Joe Pesci in Martin Scorsese's *The Irishman* would later immortalize Bufalino. Bufalino, known as the "Quiet Don," is said to have had a hand in many violent historic events, including 1961's Bay of Pigs invasion, President Kennedy's assassination, and Jimmy Hoffa's disappearance in 1975. Both singer Al Martino and actor Marlon Brando recorded in their individual memoirs that Bufalino had a curious role in the production of Francis Ford Coppola's *The Godfather*. Brando said Bufalino visited him in his trailer, and Martino wrote that he had asked Bufalino, who was his godfather, to help him land the role of Johnny Fontane. Vic Damone initially had been chosen for the role by the film's producers over Martino. Then Damone dropped out. In a weird parallel, the character Johnny Fontane, based on Frank Sinatra, asks a favor of his godfather, played by Brando, to help him land a movie role. Before he died under suspicious circumstances in 1963, William Morris agent George Wood was Vic Damone's agent as well as Frank Sinatra's. In Damone's memoir, he recounts how George Wood saved his life once, when Damone was at low point. In truth, this low point was Damone dangling from a balcony, held by his legs by mobster Joe Adonis.

For Andy, there may have been too many skeletons in his closet to run for office. I had a conversation with my teenage son, who is keenly observant of politics and wants to go into public service, about what would have happened had Andy Griffith instead of John Ingram run against Jesse Helms in 1978. Helms won that election with 54 percent of the vote and then campaigned for Ronald Reagan in 1980.

But my son suggested that if Andy had run, he would have won—it was said only two people could have beaten Jesse Helms in North Carolina, Andy Griffith and Jesus—and the entire planet would be different. Not just a small part of the world but the entire geopolitical landscape of the last forty years. Senator Griffith would have campaigned for Jimmy Carter in 1980, which may have nudged Carter over Reagan. All the Reagan policies that current society is still wrestling with the aftermath of—debt, homelessness, escalating rents and cost of living—might have been avoided. Putin might not be in power in Russia. Trump might not have bubbled up in 2016.

A way North Carolina attempted to bury its divisive past was by declaring amnesty in 1873 for the Klan and others who'd terrorized the countryside. The law included the Union resistors as well. It lists ten groups in total, and the language hints there were more. This was not a state unified behind a Lost Cause—the law exonerated "the Heroes of America, Loyal Union League, Red Strings, Constitutional Union Guard, White Brotherhood, Invisible Empire, Ku-Klux Klan, North Carolina State Troops, North Carolina Militia, Jay Hawkers, or any other organization, association or assembly, secret or otherwise, political or otherwise."

People may remember Marvel Comics' wonderful *What If?* series, which first ran from 1977 to 1984 and has been adapted for TV on Disney+, starring Jeffrey Wright. In the comic books, a mysterious narrator, Uatu the Watcher, from his perch on the moon, revealed what would have happened if some defining event in the life of a superhero hadn't occurred. Peter Parker's defining event, for instance, was that he did not stop the mugger who later murdered his beloved uncle, which was the crime-fighting catalyst for Spider-Man. But what if Peter Parker *had* stopped the mugger? All he had to do was reach out, block the door, and stop him. Well, in this alternative universe, the writers of *What If?* made Parker a vacuous late-Elvis-like celebrity, estranged from his still-living uncle (which disturbed me when I was ten). But what if North Carolina returned to that moment in 1876 and 14,001 additional people voted for Thomas Settle? Who would we be now? What if Andy Griffith had run against Jesse Helms?

I remember well the exact moment I arrived in New York. Just as I penetrated the outskirts of the miraculous city, with its million heady possibilities and bright inventions, the little car's radio picked up New York City's great jazz station, WKCR. John Coltrane's "Giant Steps" was playing. Along with Andy Griffith, Nina Simone, Michael Jordan, Doc Watson, and others, Coltrane is one of the greatest cultural figures North Carolina has produced. Of course, he left the Tar Heel State as soon as he could, as a teenager, never to return. I turned the volume up full blast, rolled down the windows, and let out one of Whitman's barbaric yawps into the blinking night. If anyone heard me, they may have thought I was happy, or perhaps angry, or aggrieved. It sounded like that.

> I too am not a bit tamed, I too am untranslatable,
> I sound my barbaric yawp over the roofs of the
> world.
> . . .
> It coaxes me to the vapor and the dusk.

In April 2011, the North Carolina Senate voted to pardon Governor William Woods Holden of any wrongdoing in the Kirk-Holden War. This was intended as a ceremonial gesture on the 140th anniversary of Holden's removal from office. The senators, however, discovered an anonymous letter on each of their desks, which, according to the *Raleigh News & Observer*, cited a hundred-year-old book accusing Holden of "running a corrupt administration and supporting carpetbaggers and scalawags." A teenage volunteer for the Caswell County Historical Association emailed his senator, "Holden never truly convicted anyone of being a member in the Ku Klux Klan. If you allow this resolution to pass . . . you will condemn Caswell's history on the state level and put us all to shame." Perhaps Holden would have agreed with the young historian. In 1873, deprived of office and commenting on absolution for the Klan and others in the insurrection, Holden wrote, "I am in favor of amnesty, oblivion, mercy to the guilty."

53.

One of the many things I did during the pandemic, in part to endure my loneliness in New England, was to watch episodes of *NC Weekend* on PBS. After I discovered that the PBS app on my Roku TV had an archive of UNC-TV's public television shows going back to the early 1990s, if I needed comforting in an empty apartment I'd keyword-search something on the PBS app related to North Carolina, like "Manteo" or "Winston-Salem," and usually an episode of *NC Weekend* would pop up. Shows representing years and years of barbecue festivals, blacksmith festivals, shad festivals, restaurant reviews with Bob Garner, historic sites, and visits to the Lost Colony and Elizabethan Gardens, and in which I got to hear the North Carolina accents of regular people and docents and tour guides and history reenactors interviewed for the TV segments, made me less homesick and lonely, and I was homesick and lonely long before the pandemic. When I lost New York City and my life there, I was sick with grief missing that, and still am, but I often wished I were in North Carolina. When asked where I would go if I could move anywhere, I often say, Back home to North Carolina, but maybe somewhere new, a place I've never lived before, like Asheville, Durham, or Wilmington. Letting PBS stream one segment after another of local programming from NC Public TV comforted me. Plus, I might get to watch Bob Garner review restaurants and enjoy his meal. (I want his job when he retires. Garner's made at least two barbecue documentaries for UNC-TV.)

On the twenty-fifth anniversary special of UNC-TV's *North Carolina People*, national news commentator Charles Kuralt, describing the reasoning behind the state's motto, Esse Quam Videri (also the show's apt subtitle), imagined the thinking of the North Carolinians who reached after that Latin phrase from Cicero when they selected it for the state seal: "After all, North Carolina people saw themselves that way.... There was a democratic plainness to the landscape. No urban life in the state to compare with Virginia. No wealthy plantations to compare with South Carolina. But everybody has to have something to be proud of, and in North Carolina, we have always been mighty proud of not being too proud. Being humble and plain. And at the same time being courageous and resourceful and gregarious."

Watching North Carolina PBS has encouraged me to fantasize about moving back home to North Carolina when my children finish high school, if I can afford to make the move.

Although, one episode of *NC Weekend* featured the courthouse at the center of the Kirk-Holden War, where the Klan murdered a man. The town historian was sweating and looked uneasy. Another town historian glibly mentioned a "carpetbagger was stabbed." I think I may know who left those anonymous notes.

54.

Throughout the 1980s, the coastal North Carolina town of Wilmington grew a Hollywood business in miniature, courting film and television productions, spurred by Andy Griffith's decision to move production of his TV series *Matlock* to Wilmington in the last years of its run. This encouraged the North Carolina School of the Arts to expand in the late '90s and open an undergraduate film school, the first of its kind in the state. Its initial graduating classes included David Gordon Green, Gregory Orr, Paul Schneider, Shawn Harwell, Danny McBride, Ben Best, and Jody Hill—and all of them found each other there, when before few had friends who shared their interests. Now, Jody Hill, Danny McBride, and David Gordon Green own a production company, Rough House, with development deals in place. Paul Schneider, raised in Asheville, who was a player on the first two seasons of *Parks and Recreation* before landing a major role in Jane Campion's *Bright Star*, has said the North Carolina School of the Arts was the only college he applied to. The screenwriter Shawn Harwell wrote me, "It was sheer luck that a film school opened up in Winston-Salem. . . . I honestly have no clue what I would be doing if they hadn't accepted me. Probably something at Western Steer."

55.

Before Sam Griffith died in the shower at a friend's house, after mixing pills and alcohol, he had shopped a book proposal for a memoir called "I'm Not Opie." Contrary to rumor, Sam did not resent Ron Howard or the relationship Andy's character, Andy Taylor, had with his son, Opie, played by Ron Howard. Sam knew that was only a TV show. Ron and his family were his dad's friends and had worked for many great years together. Andy was Sam's dad. And they had a great relationship until Sam was around fifteen or sixteen and started drinking and smoking, and then Andy didn't know what to do with him and always seemed pissed off about something. Then his mother, Barbara, died in 1980, and Sam was financially independent and did whatever he wanted. But when he was a kid, he and his dad had gone to major league baseball games, went deep-sea fishing for bluefish and marlin, played volleyball, swam, and surfed. Andy had an RV he'd drive out to the desert and dunes, and they'd camp and race motocross dirt bikes. They had a blast every summer on the beach in North Carolina—swimming and boating, big neighborhood barbecues and campfire crab boils. Along with his sister, Dixie, Sam even worked in productions of *The Lost Colony*.

Sam didn't so much like sharing his dad with millions of fans, and one time his dad had scolded him for telling fans they were in a hurry, after they had stopped Andy for an autograph in Los Angeles. "They pay our bills, Sam. Don't ever be impatient and rude." Yet Sam knew his dad tried his best to avoid being noticed by fans when he could, and if Sam was impatient and rude, where did he learn that? Sam didn't always enjoy living in his father's shadow, but he didn't resent Ron Howard. "I'm Not Opie" just seemed like a good title. Some of the chapter titles were great too. One was called "Pa and I Fish." A few others were titled "Keeping the Tourists at Bay" and "My Father and I Fight the Hurricane."

56.

It was total war. By fighter plane, battleship, destroyer, aircraft carrier, submarine, and other vessels, in both American and Japanese armadas, and by land—the first overland battle fought by the American military in World War II, led by the hastily prepared marines, First Division. It began in August 1942, not long after the Allies learned of a large airfield under construction by the Japanese on an obscure jungle-covered patch of the South Pacific called Guadalcanal in the Solomon Islands. If the Japanese military were allowed to finish the airstrip, it could cut off the supply lines between the West Coast of America and Australia and New Zealand or, worse, allow the Japanese navy to eventually work its way toward joining up with Hitler's forces.

Without proper training, supplies, a clear plan, or even an accurate map, the marines landed on Guadalcanal and took the airfield, sometimes battling inches at a time across the jungle. By mid-October they were dug in, sick from dysentery and malaria and expecting yet another onslaught from the Japanese to retake the field. The Japanese naval bombardment on October 13 and 14 dropped tons of fourteen-inch exploding shells on the marines. It was almost impossible to endure. One marine recalled when the day broke on the morning of the fourteenth, five acres of coconut trees that he'd been able to see from his tent the day before were gone. Just gone.

At this moment, a baby-faced, skinny twenty-three-year-old marine corporal named Paul Linke Jr. from New

Jersey (his friends called him Bobby) left his mates to make his way to the pillboxes by Henderson Field to play his horn for the marines holding the front line. Paul was the ship's bugler aboard the recently built USS *North Carolina*. There was a break in the shelling, and Bobby thought the familiar sound of his horn, maybe some jazz, would lift their spirits and help them keep up the fight.

Before joining the marines in 1940, before Pearl Harbor, Bobby had been the drummer in the Jan Savitt Orchestra and played dance halls across New Jersey and Pennsylvania, mostly in Philadelphia. In 1940, when he saw the way the war in Europe was going and knew that America would be forced to join the fray, he joined the marines. They had the best band. Plus, his father, Paul Sr., was a German immigrant, and he wanted to demonstrate his family's loyalty. Before he shipped out, he was stationed at Cape May and then at Paris Island, and finally, before leaving for the Solomon Islands, he trained in North Carolina for amphibious landings on the Cape Fear River outside Wilmington. His ship, the USS *North Carolina*, was the most powerful ship in the world, built and outfitted in the Brooklyn Naval Yard the year Bobby joined the service. Walter Winchell called the USS *North Carolina* "the Showboat," after the Broadway show. Somehow Winchell knew that Bobby was the bugler and had played with Jan Savitt and mentioned it in one of his columns. Bobby wondered whether his older brother Dick had something to do with the squib. Dick worked in New York City and hung out at the same bars and clubs that Winchell went to. Maybe Dick had slipped it in somehow, as a favor.

57.

In an article for the *Saturday Evening Post* in 1964, Andy's personal manager and business partner, Dick Linke, bragged to the reporter that he had introduced the starstruck Andy Griffith to Frank Sinatra at Danny's Hideway in the 1950s, a famous midtown bar and restaurant in New York City and celebrity hangout. This wasn't the first time he'd told this story in an attempt to build up his brand and expand his client base. At the same time, the profile intended to add dimension to Andy's cachet, looking ahead for life after *The Andy Griffith Show*. In the piece, Andy admitted to having a brooding social anxiety and a quick and monstrous temper. It also featured a photo of him sweating on a tractor, wearing a formfitting work shirt, seeding a row of cedar on his Manteo estate's tree farm. The publicity firm of Rogers & Cowan had signed off on the interview. Andy's management team was hoping for larger, more dynamic leading roles for Andy in movies and thinking that the actor was in serious danger of being typecast and limited to rural TV comedy roles the rest of his career.

By 1964, when Dick Linke name-dropped Sinatra to the *Saturday Evening Post*, Sinatra had been singing for three decades, and his star had risen and fallen more than once. It was one of these dips in Sinatra's career, in the early 1950s, after a painful divorce, a volatile relationship with Ava Gardner, and several suicide attempts, that Sinatra found himself without sold-out shows and cut loose from his record label. In 1953, Sinatra gambled on a move to upstart Capitol Records. It was a fortunate play for Sinatra, and at Capitol's state-of-the-art studios in Los Angeles he created some of his greatest albums, with Nelson Riddle conducting. Nelson Riddle was also the conductor for Capitol's best-selling artist, Nat King Cole. When Sinatra first heard the playback after recording with Riddle, he famously exclaimed, "I'm back, baby, I'm back!" Had Frank Sinatra not made this bet on Capitol, we'd not have such great albums as "In the Wee Small Hours" and "Come Fly with Me"—and, also, we might not remember Andy Griffith, as it was the Sinatra deal with Capitol that helped introduce Andy Griffith to the wide world.

In 1953, when the arrangement between Sinatra and Capitol was in the works with Abe Lastfogel's boys at the William Morris Agency, not long after Hal Cook at Capitol purchased the Colonial Records master recording from Andy and Colonial's owner, Orville Campbell, and the seven-inch vinyl of "What It Was, Was Football" was flying out of the record bins across America, an executive at Capitol suggested to his counterpart at William Morris that they have a look at Andy Griffith.

Dick Linke met Andy on the sidewalk outside of the William Morris offices, where Andy was looking up at the Mutual of New York office building on Fifty-Sixth Street and Seventh Avenue, the skyscraper a few blocks south of Central Park. That building was gleaming and new, topped with a giant neon sign that read "Mutual of New York," with the first letter of each word flashing in giant red letters: MONY. Andy shook his head, took a drag on his cigarette, and said, "Well I'll be damned."

Andy had signed an unheard-of artist management agreement with Capitol, which put him on salary. So it was in Capitol's best interests to look out for Andy's best interests. He and Dick were there to meet with George Wood, who was the head of the East Coast office—and Sinatra's manager, among other things. Then after, they'd meet Abe Lastfogel, the head of the agency, and his wife, Frances Arms. They lived in a permanent suite at Essex House.

George Wood was dapper and classy, wore flashy clothes and jewelry—including a thin Swiss wristwatch that cost more than Andy's car—and liked to pepper his speech with colorful phrasing, such as words like "cocksucker." Wood was a gambler, rumored to be the front man for the mob in the entertainment business, and under investigation by more than one law enforcement agency. "You'll be headlining at clubs across America," Dick had assured Andy. But Andy left the meeting nervous and worried. Only a year before he'd been teaching schoolchildren in North Carolina and singing in church. Andy was right to have been nervous. Vincent "Jimmy Blue Eyes" Alo was best man at Wood's wedding. Alo was a capo in the Genovese family, the crime family started by Lucky Luciano. Jimmy Blue Eyes was an associate of Frank Costello, Joe Adonis, and Meyer Lansky. Immortalized in *The Godfather Part II*, the stand-in for Alo is Johnny Ola's character. Wood was reportedly beaten bloody at the Camelot Lounge on Forty-Ninth Street a few years later and died the next day at a New York hospital. After Georgie died, Jimmy Alo paid Wood's $100,000 in gambling debts. Frank Costello was among the mourners who attended Wood's funeral.

Andy told Dick and the other executives at Capitol Records that he was happy for William Morris to represent him, but he didn't want to have George Wood as his agent—that made him too jumpy. Wood's boss, Abe Lastfogel, the president of the company—whom his clients called Uncle Abe and who had started working at the talent agency at the age of fourteen, running errands for Mr. Morris—signed Andy as a client. The dignified Harry Kalcheim would assist. Harry wore ugly brown suits.

Dick Linke didn't know what it was about this young man from North Carolina. He had a star quality. Magnetic. Electric. But it was something else too. Andy was earnest and hardworking and had a big, easy laugh. He reminded Dick a bit of his kid brother Bobby, just a year younger than Dick, who had died in action during the war. Andy was musical, played the horn, and loved jazz, just like Bobby. Maybe it was a sign. Bobby had served aboard the USS *North Carolina* and had trained down there along the Cape Fear River and had shipped out from North Carolina, gone through the canal, and sailed on to the Solomon Islands, where a Japanese mortar shell killed him. The last part of America that Bobby had stood on while he was alive was North Carolina. Whatever the reason, Dick wanted to look after Andy. Their stars were aligned.

58.

In 1918, during the height of the global Spanish flu pandemic, Frederich Henry Koch arrived in Chapel Hill, North Carolina. He was a young Ohio Wesleyan graduate who'd grown up in Peoria, Illinois, the son of an accountant. Koch was a thespian and had completed graduate work at Harvard. In the years after college, he'd traveled the country reciting Shakespeare at train stations and guild halls and community playhouses and would have loved to continue acting and reciting poetry until the end of his days, but to satisfy the demands of his accountant father and the basic human need for food and shelter, in a scant and competitive teaching market Koch used his master's degree from Harvard to land a job teaching in the lonesome wilds of America's interior, at the University of North Dakota. Koch had free rein to create a fledgling dramatic arts program.

An English instructor Koch had studied with at Harvard, the innovative George Pierce Baker, had profoundly influenced Koch. Baker had created a unique playwriting workshop in which students wrote plays and performed them as part of the program of study. It had never before been done at Harvard—in three centuries of that storied institution's existence. An early student of Baker's was Eugene O'Neill. Harvard wasn't able to keep Baker, however. George Pierce Baker unsuccessfully lobbied Harvard to offer a degree in drama, and when the old institution declined, he left for the greener pastures of Yale and helped found the Yale School of Drama.

In North Dakota, Professor Koch labored for several years, expanded on his old professor's methods, and developed a curriculum in which the drama students wrote and produced plays based on the real people they knew in life, which he called folk plays. The students would then travel the Dakota countryside holding up this social mirror, performing the folk dramas for the folks they were writing about. He called the group the Dakota Playmakers.

Koch's innovative work gained press attention nationally, and in 1918 the head of the University of North Carolina, Edward Kidder Graham, sent a letter to Koch and lured the drama teacher to the oldest public state university in America, the University of North Carolina at Chapel Hill. Koch brought his program in which students created and produced and acted in one-act folk dramas and established the Carolina Playmakers in a region rich in folk history and storytelling. The program took root immediately and prospered. Koch's first male acting student, in 1918, was a tall young man from Asheville, North Carolina, Thomas Wolfe. Later, with Koch's encouragement, Wolfe went to Harvard and studied with George Pierce Baker.

In 1922, the Playmakers' aim was codified in the first edition of *Carolina Folk-Plays*, published by Henry Holt and Company:

> First: To promote and encourage dramatic
> art, especially by the production and
> publishing of plays.

Second: To serve as an experimental theatre
for the development of plays representing
the traditions and various phases of
present-day life of the people.

Third: To extend its influences in the
establishment of a native theatre in other
communities.

In his instruction, Koch anticipates William Carlos
Williams's notion of the universal local. He writes, "The
locality, if it be truly interpreted, is the only universal. It
has been so in all lasting literature. And in every locality
all over America, as here in North Carolina to-day, there
is the need and the striving for a fresh expression of our
common folk life."

59.

Meanwhile, two decades earlier in New York City, a young German Jewish man, who'd been born Zelman Moses in Germany and had immigrated to New York with his parents when he was nine years old, anglicized his name to William Morris and wandered Manhattan, transfixed by the majesty of it all. On days off from his job as a clerk, he strolled past dozens of vaudeville theaters, dime museums, and beer halls that dotted the landscape—along the Bowery, over on Second Avenue, as far up as Union Square, and as far east as Avenue B. Morris lingered at freak shows and clapped with delight for singers, mystics, comedians, acrobats, fire breathers, and bearded ladies. Ambitious, well liked, and determined to be a part of the multiheaded machine that entertained his country, William Morris in 1893 used letterhead he somehow acquired from the M. B. Leavitt talent agency and used it to compose a letter to Leavitt's competitor, the George Liman Agency, requesting a position. Liman hired him. Five years later, in 1898, after Liman died and his widow took over the business and fired Morris, William Morris hung his shingle at a newly rented office directly across the street, on Fourteenth Street. By 1909, Morris opened an office in Chicago. In 1914, he hired an office boy named Abe Lastfogel, who, through a program for underprivileged youth, had been handed two slips of paper with addresses at which to apply for a job and picked one at random. And by 1953, Abe Lastfogel was running the William Morris Agency, with offices in New York, Chicago,

London, Paris, Rome, Madrid, and Beverly Hills. By 1955, the venerable old agency represented, among others, Mae West, Jimmy Durante, Fanny Brice, Danny Thomas, Frank Sinatra, Count Basie, Danny Kaye, Glenn Ford, Richard Wright, Martha Raye, Rita Hayworth, Marilyn Monroe, and Elvis—and, thanks to Capitol Records, Andy Griffith. By 1960, when *The Andy Griffith Show* aired, at the apex of what are known as packaging deals, meaning an agency would supply every component of a TV show or movie—actors, writers, producers, directors, and so on— the William Morris Agency was responsible for packaging twenty-seven hours of programming on American television every week.

60.

Judging by the number of plaques and badges presented to Andy Griffith by local sheriffs' associations across America, many county sheriffs imagine they are following after the model character of Andy Taylor on *The Andy Griffith Show*. They grew up watching the show and were influenced to serve the community and harass the bad guys and care for their loved ones. One sheriff above all others, for good or ill, has become famous for his nononsense approach to policing and for his press conferences conducted like seminars in the nuances of southern storytelling: Sheriff Grady Judd of Polk County, Florida. His press reports and video news interviews posted on YouTube have several million views. For monetized channels, at the moment YouTube pays about five dollars per thousand views, so it's possible Grady Judd's articulations and crime reports are a money machine. The local news channels have compiled "That's So Grady" montages of Gradyisms. In one video on his YouTube channel, Judd indicates that he became a sheriff directly because of his love for *The Andy Griffith Show*, and he also acknowledges that he is sometimes compared to Barney Fife. Judd is indeed way more of a Barney. It seems he cares very much for the shiny emblems of his office—four silver stars on each collar of his uniform; a Batman utility belt; a variety of black uniform styles, with gold stitching, for all occasions; and his own gold-trimmed county sheriff's flag standing tall behind him at press conferences, beside the Stars and Stripes and the state flag of Florida. Judd is an enigmatic figure and earned his popularity—he is a gifted storyteller and presents cases against the accused as if they are already convicted criminals and he is in a courtroom drama speaking to a rapt jury. Judd does not seem to imagine that anyone would have a reason for attempting to enter a stranger's house or car other than for criminal intent.

For the majority of the pandemic, Judd and his deputies did not wear masks to protect themselves or the public, and when questioned by reporters about this he refused to answer or simply said that when President Trump visited, he did not wear a mask. Judd has been sheriff since 2004 and has waded into the political waters. He has met with Trump, and Judd's endorsement of Representative Scott Franklin in the 2020 Florida election, along with now disgraced Matt Gaetz's support, helped Franklin win his seat. Yet Judd, immediately after the George Floyd killing, told the public that if that incident had happened in his county, he would have put the deputies in jail immediately, and in truth, he has arrested and fired his own officers for various offenses, including making threats against the Capitol after the January 6, 2021, insurrection. Grady Judd arrested a six-year veteran for messaging a coworker that the FBI was corrupt and the streets of Washington, DC, should run red with the blood of tyrants.

Polk County, Florida, is certainly not Mayberry. Some of the crimes mentioned in the many press conferences on YouTube put together by the county or local news outlets or directly by the sheriff's office include the stealing of heads from the bodies of entombed people in graveyards, a revenge killing over a stolen truck, and the killing of a classmate's mom by a group of teenagers who ran her over with a church van. In the last instance, Judd convinced the district attorney to try the children as adults and did not seem to think anything was dangerous or wrong about posting the faces and names of the minors involved in the incident, when one was a fourteen-year-old girl who clearly had just gotten in the van with her friends. After one of Judd's deputies was shot and killed at a traffic stop and the other deputies shot the killer sixty-eight times, a reporter asked whether Judd thought that was an excessive number of bullets. Judd famously replied, "That's all the bullets we had, or we would have shot him more." Online, there is merchandise available for sale, T-shirts, baseball caps, and pandemic face masks that read, "God Guns Grady Judd." No punctuation.

61.

In all possible universes there is at least one where Andy Griffith didn't take up the trombone, didn't study music with Reverend Ed Mickey, didn't decide to be a Moravian minister, didn't go to the University of North Carolina, didn't walk past the back of the Playmakers Theatre and spy the audition notice for Gilbert and Sullivan's *Gondoliers*, didn't take the summer job on Roanoke Island acting in *The Lost Colony* and instead made a little bit more money working at the furniture factory with his dad. In that reality, Andy stayed there, working on the same factory floor as his father, making high-end solid wood furniture, employed by the Mount Airy Chair Company until it merged with the Mount Airy Furniture Company in 1966, and then, in 1997, a few years after Andy retired, the factory burned to the ground. Andy volunteered to help with the cleanup and marveled at all that had been lost.

And in yet another universe, Andy is remembered as a cautionary tale told to college freshmen, a tragic music student who fell asleep with a lit cigarette and died in a consuming fire in Battle Hall on the UNC campus. There is a fading brass plaque in the lobby and a scholarship in his name offered by his classmates. In another universe, Andy makes a hit record in 1953 but never meets Dick Linke, and Andy's original recording sells great. Still, instead of Andy touring nightclubs incessantly across the country in 1954 and signing with William Morris, Andy struggles a few years to find a foothold but moves to New York City and eventually breaks into Broadway with the help and encouragement of his wife and friends, and by the late 1960s he establishes himself as a reliable character actor. After a fifty-year career, Andy's IMDb page lists over 300 films and TV shows, including several films with his good friend Bob Armstrong. He, along with Bob, is a favorite of Sam Peckinpah and Warren Beatty, and the highlight of Andy's career is the win of a Best Supporting Oscar for his role in Beatty's 1981 film, *Reds*. Andy Griffith wins over John Gielgud, Ian Holm, Howard E. Rollins Jr., and James Coco and delivers one of the most memorable acceptance speeches in Academy history. Clips of it are played in every montage of famous acceptance speeches forty years later, along with those of Sally Field, Halle Berry, Roberto Benigni, and Tom Hanks.

In another dimension of the Andy Griffith multiverse, Andy and Barbara refuse to borrow money to print a brochure or to leave their jobs to go on the road and perform and instead stay in Goldsboro and teach schoolchildren, and they sing at church and live out their lives quietly in Goldsboro, taking great pride in their students and always tuning into NPR to hear their former student Carl Kasell.

There is a universe where, after five great seasons, in 1965, Andy does not renew his contract with CBS, and *The Andy Griffith Show* ceases production. Andy defies the wishes of his powerful agent and head of the William Morris Agency, Abe Lastfogel, and asks to be cut in to the five-picture deal with Don Knotts at Universal, as co-lead. He and Don make the two top-grossing comedies of the decade and reunite in the 1970s for a set of films for Disney. Andy is cast as the lead in Hal Ashby's *Being There* in

1979, and for the rest of his days people shout, "Chauncey Gardner!" when they encounter Andy at airports.

But none of those realities is our reality. They all could have happened, and in all possible universes each did happen in at least one. Yet our Andy was driven and ambitious, and he shaped and created his own destiny, although it must have been dizzying at times to see how far he had gone so fast, and he might have wondered which thread, if pulled, would make everything unravel. His success was so immediate and full right from the beginning, landing a leading role in a feature film with a top director in his very first film, *A Face in the Crowd*. In interviews for over fifty years, Andy often remarked on how his initial success all happened, as if it were by accident. At the beginning, in 1957, Edward R. Murrow offered that question, asking Andy if one had to be lucky, in the right place at the right time, and Andy answered thoughtfully, nodding, yes, there is luck involved, but you have to have some talent and be ready when luck finds you.

62.

The idea was simple and elegant, and not altogether new: Andy's face made giant, gracing a chain of restaurants serving generally typical southern fare, and specifically North Carolina–style barbecue. Andy's smiling face on the giant sign by the highway. Andy's toothy maw on the polystyrene cups, the laminated menu, the paper placemats. Andy's mug on a line of canned vegetables and beans in grocery stores. A cartoon drawing of his grinning, lined face, his teeth maybe drawn slightly enlarged and out of proportion, as if he's about to devour the words "Good eatin'."

Andy's partners included former North Carolina governor Terry Sanford and Harry Stewart Jr., the former director of dining halls at North Carolina State University, which fed thousands of students and faculty daily. The test restaurant was in Raleigh. The idea wasn't innovative. Others had succeeded in this market. Singer Jimmy Dean successfully cashed in his fame from the hit song "Big John" and made a move into the food business, hawking country sausage and biscuits. Cowboy film star Roy Rogers capitalized on the fast-food craze of the 1950s and '60s, selling his good name to a chain of burger joints.

63.

Up until this moment in my life, in all my years on earth, I have failed at everything I've attempted. My dreams of success in sports were dashed as a kid, I launched a failed business just out of college, my work as a writer stalled just as it began, I have a novel in my desk drawer and several unsold screenplays, my friendships are scattered and frayed, my marriage blew up in a public and humiliating way. All my many romantic relationships since have been more or less failures. My second career as an editor and a freelance writer stalled and sputtered in the wreckage of my marriage. I missed a few deadlines and thought better of burning more bridges with editors, and so I stopped pitching. My plans of writing for film and TV never panned out. I decided to lose twenty pounds last August and instead gained seven. I have a pillowcase filled with rejections in the back of my closet. I now make less money each year than I did twenty years ago. For years now I've steadily applied for mid- and entry-level corporate jobs since I left New York City and can count my in-person interviews on two hands. I work fifty-three hours a week as a clerk in a grocery store and editing obituaries for a local newspaper group and sometimes have to sell my belongings to pay for dinner with my kids or put gas in the seventeen-year-old car I drive. Yet the lesson I gather from the life of Andy Griffith is you never stop; there's never success without failure. You keep going. You fail until you succeed. As Samuel Beckett wrote, "Ever tried. Ever failed. No matter. Try again. Fail again. Fail better."

64.

Not long into the interview, the young journalist asked Andy what it was like growing up in Mount Airy. Andy was approaching eighty, and the long interview was intended to be comprehensive, about his entire career, and for the ages. Andy hesitated and looked at his wife Cindi, who sat across the room, there to help if he stumbled over a memory, as she knew most all the stories about his career that he told reporters. He smiled, looked at the reporter with his head slightly cocked, and with a light in his eye, mulling over his response, he said, "I felt second-class my whole childhood."

65.

Once the cab crossed Houston Street, Andy looked out the back window, as the unfamiliar city became even more unfamiliar. The numbered streets disappeared, replaced by strange names. The grid pattern gave way to narrow blocks and bends and curves. He'd been in the Village enough, at clubs, at dinner and drinks, and at friends' apartments, that he could find his way to Sixth Avenue if needed, but across town, on the Lower East Side, this was new territory for the North Carolina boy. The cab pulled over at Kenmare; the guitar shifted in Andy's lap. Supposedly this guy was the best. He's asked around, and more than one musical friend said the same. The neat little guitar shop was marked with his name, D'Angelico. Inside the shop, John D'Angelico's projects were mounted on the wall, hanging from hooks from the ceiling like hogs in a butcher shop.

66.

On April 14, 2014, I left New York City. I could not afford to hire movers and was too embarrassed to ask my friends to help. I joked about it with one or two, but, understandably, since my friends and I were in our mid-forties, with careers and families, no one was eager to assist. I tried to sell the few things I couldn't carry by myself, and when that didn't happen I left the items in our NYC co-op, which was in my ex-wife's name—mainly a Ted Boerner Theatre sofa from Design Within Reach, which was attractive but not terribly comfortable or cozy, and giant Reve bed with a king-size memory foam mattress. The bed frame and mattress were crazily expensive, even on sale, and every time in the following years I woke stiff on the floor after sleeping on my daughter's twin bedroll from IKEA, or had no money for gas or food, I thought of that damn bed. I should have asked someone to help me with the mattress, but then I would have needed help every time I moved. And I moved so many more times, and likely will keep moving, who knows. When I packed the rented U-Haul that day, I imagined I was setting out for a new life in Massachusetts, with no idea what would happen, other than I would be a father to my children. I had lived in that NYC apartment for sixteen years. The Boston region was completely alien to me, but how hard could it be? I had managed to make a life for myself in NYC, coming from a small town in North Carolina. Often we make the worst mistakes for the right reasons. Often we are unlucky. E. B. White famously wrote in his anonymous guidebook for the WPA, *This Is New York*, that if you move to New York City you have to be willing to be lucky. And I was. But when I left NYC I was unwilling to be unlucky. Yet I was unlucky.

Andy Griffith left North Carolina for New York City, then left New York City for coastal North Carolina, then left coastal North Carolina for Los Angeles but spent summers and holidays in North Carolina, then larger chunks of the year, and then eventually left Los Angeles entirely.

The custodian of the building I lived in, Oleg, was kind to my children and dedicated to his job. He'd been a naval commander in pre-1989 Russia. After he saw me stacking boxes by the elevator in the hallway, Oleg let me borrow an old luggage cart to roll my belongings from my apartment to the truck. My things had mostly been packed up for months, as I'd wanted to move for months, yet I did not have a job in Massachusetts or a place to live.

67.

Originally, Andy planned on attending a small Moravian college in Pennsylvania to prepare for the ministry. Music had changed his life, had given him more confidence and a sense of purpose—the attention and praise of his peers and elders. Reverend Mickey taught him as much as he was willing to learn. And he wanted to learn everything there was to know about musical instruments. He began with the trombone—the one he'd ordered from the Spiegel catalog with the money he'd earned sweeping the high school, a job that was funded as part of FDR's New Deal. So in following this trajectory, which began with getting the job sweeping floors, he imagined a life like Reverend Mickey's, conducting the band and the chorus, playing music, leading a flock of Moravian churchgoers. Andy often said if that had happened—if he had attended the little Moravian college in Pennsylvania—he'd have become a bad preacher instead of an entertainer. He often said a lot of things, again and again. He was fiercely private, protecting an image crafted and honed over decades. "Go-oo-ood cracker." He told the same stories to reporters and talk show hosts in hundreds of interviews and appearances. Condensed versions based on one version of reality. Leaving out chunks of time and machinations and failed projects and confrontations and some of the names and faces involved in the process but hitting the larger notes and staying generally true enough. Some tinges of bitterness, revenge. He told the story of rejection at the playhouse in New Jersey, which was conflated with New York, his first professional audition, after which the casting director basically told him his singing voice was painful to listen to. He told the story of bombing on *Ed Sullivan* when he first arrived in New York, his first appearance on television, and getting fired. Of Abe Lastfogel sending him off to work the clubs and learn how to entertain and be funny. Anecdotes of hearing someone whistling *The Andy Griffith Show* theme music at every airport across the world by someone behind him in line, an unsubtle clue that he'd been recognized. Varying versions of the story of why he continued *The Andy Griffith Show* after Don Knotts left, of why he and Don didn't do movies together, of why Don left the show. Of CBS's "rural purge" by Mike Dann. It was rare for a newspaper reporter or a magazine writer or a talk show host to draw a new version of a story out of Andy, or a new story at all. This was in large part a learned practice of manager Dick Linke. He discussed talking points ahead of time with talk show producers and his clients—the stable of entertainers he managed, with Andy Griffith at its center. Nothing was exactly a lie and nothing was entirely true. Andy could have gone after a career like Gregory Peck's or Walter Matthau's, but after a queasy dramatic turn on *Playhouse 90* and the failure of *Onionhead*, Dick Linke was hypervigilant about Andy's crafted persona. In 1969, Andy's attempt to break back into movies as a sympathetic leading man with *Angel in My Pocket* fell flat. *Angel in My Pocket* was the first film in a canceled five-film contract with Universal, which followed the monster success of *The Andy Griffith Show*. This was the opposite of what happened for Don Knotts. After the death of *The Andy Griffith Show* and Andy's three dismal failures in a row, the forgettable film and two failed series, it wasn't until the early 1970s that Andy reinvented himself as a villain and found a niche in hour-long TV melodramas. Dick Linke tightly held the reins of Andy's career from the beginning. It only gradually began to relax, and then eventually, in 1991, Andy parted ways with Dick Linke entirely. Neither man spoke on the record about what happened.

68.

Angel in My Pocket was supposed to appeal to his base; he used the best writers from *The Andy Griffith Show,* the same writers who wrote those hits for Don Knotts. Don was doing great on the big screen, but it seemed to Andy that people didn't want him on the big screen. They didn't want to pay a buck and a quarter for admission and two dollars for a tub of popcorn and sit in the dark to see him. The wanted him for free, in their living room. But he had to get out of the sheriff's uniform, be taken seriously. He'd heard the critics say *The Andy Griffith Show* was toothless and ignored race and the youth and all the things that were going on in the country. So he put together *Headmaster,* and it was going to tackle tough subjects and have a diverse cast, and he would be a working-class southerner who'd worked his way up the education ladder and was in charge of a private high school. They got smart young writers who were plugged in to what was going on with the kids in the country; Carl Reiner's boy Rob was one. Linda Ronstadt sang the opening theme song. It was called "Only a Man." A great song. But no one wanted to see the show. It was canned midseason. So they got the gang back together—called in Aaron Ruben to produce, hired the best writers from *The Andy Griffith Show,* and invited the old cast to make guest appearances—and put the show in another pretend town in North Carolina, gave him a pretty wife in Lee Meriwether and two blond kids this time, and pulled the strings at William Morris and built a whole episode around Glen Campbell coming to town. But fewer people watched *The New Andy Griffith Show* than *Headmaster,* so it was canceled. Then in the summer, the network ran the half-season reruns of *Headmaster* again. Andy buried both shows. After *Onionhead,* and then *Angel in My Pocket,* no one offered movie roles. None he heard about.

69.

I took the train from Penn Station in Manhattan to Raleigh, North Carolina, magically thinking that by not flying as planned and saving the venerable literary and historical organization the cost of an airline ticket, it would kick in to help me pay for another few nights in a hotel near the University of North Carolina campus, on the Durham side of town. I hadn't asked, but I thought once we all met each other and had a few drinks we'd be fast friends, and I'd mention it when I submitted the travel receipts. On the nine-hour train ride to the downtown depot in Raleigh, I read Geoff Dyer's *Out of Sheer Rage*, watched Marvel's *The Avengers* (as it was the only movie I owned), scrolled through Twitter, and rehearsed and revised a twenty-three-page informal discussion on Andy Griffith that I'd been rehearsing all week—all my talking points on the screen of the slideshow. I chose twenty-three for obvious reasons. I wanted to be lucky. I was in North Carolina. And since this was a room full of academics, I didn't want to simply read an essay. I wanted to entertain. Multimedia. Flashy and state of the art.

The evening did not go as I hoped. First the hotel computer failed, and I was moved to be last on the schedule of speakers, when the room was weary and bright and hot. Then the projector failed. You may be asking, "Evan, you had a folded copy of a short backup speech/essay in the inside of your jacket, right?" I did not. I easily could have, and I could have killed with it, even at the end when everyone was tired and irritable. I did not have a copy. I am that optimistic.

What was meant to be an informal slideshow and fun conversation at the beginning of an awards ceremony turned into a stone-sober improvised bit of stammering and insane rambling at the tail end of a sober awards dinner. I think at one point I was gurgling and bubbles were coming out of my mouth. I thought I might be having a stroke. My date couldn't stop laughing. At least I entertained one person.

At the conclusion of my ridiculous presentation, the only words spoken to me by any of the spectators in witness to the worst speech in the 100-year history of the literary society were from a lady who looked a lot like my mom, rest her soul, who got in my face with a pointed "Bless your heart!" I took it to mean go fuck yourself you idiot, we paid you and you ruined the evening. You asshat.

Regardless, I was being reimbursed for the ticket, and I didn't have enough money for a flight and extra nights in a hotel room. I stayed one night in the big Sheraton in downtown Raleigh, where the event was held, and my date and I drank a bottle of bourbon and laughed until dawn. Then I found the cheapest motel I could find off Franklin Street in Chapel Hill on the far side of town.

It was a long walk to campus but close enough that I didn't need a car, and in my days there, I had the good fortune to pass Sunrise Biscuits every morning. On foot, I would get in line behind a car, another car behind me, and walk up to the window, order a ham biscuit, and then greedily eat the biscuit on my walk to campus. I stopped doing this, getting in line with the cars, when I realized there was a walk-up window. Bless my heart, indeed.

70.

I was feeding my kids dinner at Two Boots Pizza, in the short-lived but glorious period of time when that mini-chain owned a shop on Grand Street, which corresponded with the span of my children's lives when they asked for pizza almost every day. Two Boots, as a business, began in the East Village by a husband-and-wife team and gradually expanded its empire across town to the Village, and Los Angeles, and Grand Central Station, and elsewhere. It was an eclectic, cool, eccentric brand, named Two Boots because Louisiana and Italy are both shaped like boots. The pizzas had corn meal in the crust, and toppings offered were typical Louisiana fare, like andouille, Cajun shrimp, and crawfish. It may sound gimmicky, but in the discerning and ubiquitous pizza culture that is New York City, it worked. It was great. At one point, Two Boots owned two restaurants, a video store, a movie theater, and a comedy club, all in my neighborhood, on Avenue A. About half the childhood photos of my kids eating dinner are at Two Boots, so we were thrilled when they opened on Grand Street, which is where I lived for sixteen years. It was a true joy, after trudging eastward home down that wide promenade, toward the river, after a day running errands, on the bus, wrangling kids, to pass Two Boots and discover friends waving and gesturing for you to come on inside and join them and their kids.

But in this particular moment, I was alone with my kids, and the restaurant was relatively empty. It was late in the afternoon. A few feet away was a group of teenagers from the neighborhood, high school kids, two girls and a boy, and I couldn't help but listen to their conversation. They were discussing pizza etiquette—the proper way to hold a slice and the like.

"Do you ever see people walking down the street eating a slice? Who does that. That's so gross."

"White trash," a young man answers.

71.

So much time has passed since I began the undertaking of this book that no one asks me about it anymore. People assume that either it is no longer viable or it was published and quickly forgotten, and in the hurly-burly of their lives they missed its announcement, the unboxing video on Instagram, and all the detritus of social posts and media coverage. In the years since this book began, young people have started and finished college and grad school, married and had children, divorced, subscribed to memberships at Costco and then canceled them, let their credit cards lapse. Many of my sources reached the end of their lives before the book was completed: Betty Lynn, Rance Howard, Beverly Bentley, Jerry Van Dyke, Dick Linke, Maggie Peterson, Don Rickles, and too many others.

My subject has been slippery. Andy was a man with a cultivated story, a convex mirror. He was a pitchman and protected his reputation. During his career, he had General Mills to worry about. Ritz Crackers. He had a well of pat and standard stories that he drew from that tasted the same again and again, the same questions in interviews again and again. He sold his biography to a publisher but then never completed the project. There were things he did not want to talk about. There were things his management did not want him to discuss. He didn't go off book too often. And his friends respected his privacy, except for the few who didn't. "There are things I know about Andy Griffith I'll take to my grave," a friend of Andy's son, Sam, told me. "I loved the man." His dedicated friends loved him, some of his colleagues were frightened of him, and a few who had business dealings with him despised him. This isn't unusual for a long life in the public eye, with intense amounts of capital on the line. One actor, working as an extra on *Matlock*, told me she was instructed not to make eye contact with Andy or she'd be fired. Billy Bob Thornton remembered trying to tell Andy how much he loved *The Andy Griffith Show*, growing up a troubled kid in Arkansas, after he landed a speaking role on *Matlock*, and when Billy Bob approached him, Andy grunted and stormed off. One local recalled that Andy paid the Manteo High School music teacher's salary for years and bought the band all their instruments and uniforms. Another remembered Andy as rude at a gas station. Still, those who loved him loved him enormously. His first producer from *The Andy Griffith Show*, Aaron Ruben, named his son after Andy.

After the success of Thornton's *Sling Blade* (1996), Andy called Billy Bob, and they became fast friends. Thornton cast Andy in his third film, *Daddy and Them* (2001), which had an all-star cast, including Laura Dern, Jamie Lee Curtis, John Prine, Walton Goggins, Diane Ladd, and Ben Affleck. Then Harvey Weinstein or some other monster at Miramax didn't release the film in theaters, sending it straight to the video bins. In Thornton's film, Andy plays his character's father. In *Under the Influence* (1986), Andy played Keanu Reeves's father, and for more than sixty years, he appeared, daily, on *The Andy Griffith Show*, Andy played Ron Howard's father. Howard revealed in his collaborative memoir, *The Boys*, that Andy was sterile, following a childhood bout with the mumps. Andy adopted two children and became America's surrogate father. *The Boys*, written by Ron and his brother, Clint, is about growing up in the entertainment industry and being raised by their parents, Rance and Jean, who were Andy's good friends. Andy spoke at Jean's memorial service in the fall of 2000—flying to California still recovering from a heart attack and subsequent quadruple bypass surgery earlier that summer. "That's the kind of friend Andy was," Rance Howard said. "He played an enormous role in our lives."

Jeff Bridges said of Andy, "I always hold Andy in a fond place in my heart. Respecting him as an actor as well as a human being. I consider myself lucky to have gotten to play with him."

At Mayberry Days in 2012, three months after Andy died, Ron Howard shared his thoughts about Andy Griffith at a memorial event:

Andy's impact on my life and my approach to my work really can't be measured. The balance that he sustained between focused, creative effort and this overt, playful enjoyment that he got out of working hard with people that he liked, doing a show he loved, was something that I hope I'll always remember and emulate. He helped me to understand that high achievement and leadership require confidence, yes, hard work, absolutely. But it could be gained while still maintaining humility, humanity, and a joyous appreciation for those around him.

72.

The strangest things have happened during this pandemic year, here at the close of this story. I have my children now most all the time. I went from seeing them every day of their lives to being torn away when my domestic life exploded around the time this book began. Not being in my children's daily lives, combined with everything else that was happening, sent me spiraling down so far that I've only in recent years begun to find my way out. Then, in the midst of the pandemic, I became a full-time parent again. I don't always have both my kids simultaneously, but usually one or the other is here with me in the charming, physically beautiful little town of Ipswich, Massachusetts, where sometimes people smile and say hello on the street. I live near the train, and my oldest is an independent teenager who takes the train back and forth to Cambridge, so I am not in the car as much as I once was. However, driving is more pleasant now, as I traded in the seventeen-year-old car for a newer car, only five years old. It's a Mazda and fun to drive, and I rarely eat inside it, in an attempt to keep it shiny and clean and maintained. I'm trying not to let things fall apart. The kids and I love our tiny apartment in an ancient building at the town center. I can barely afford it, and it's the ugliest building on the nicest street, but we joke about it. And it's safe and warm and home. Plus, there's a town beach nearby we can go to in the summer for free, and now that pandemic restrictions are lifting, we can walk to the YMCA where we have a family membership; it has an outdoor pool. Plus the town has lots of restaurants and breweries. I may have a beer outside sometime soon to celebrate. I try not to think of all that I lost but of all that I have. Come visit.

My son texted me tonight from his mom's house and told me he sang lullabies to his baby sister, the same songs I sang to my kids every night for years, mainly "Church in the Wildwood," which I first heard on *The Andy Griffith Show*, on the episode "Man in a Hurry." It's my favorite episode of the show and my favorite song. I texted back to him, "What a good big brother you are." And he answered that with, "Nah, I just had a good father." We live close to the Ipswich River, which has bass that can be fished—catch and release. All the three of us have to do, my kids and me, is grab some fishing poles and bait and walk down to the water, whistling.

FADE TO:
END

ACKNOWLEDGMENTS

Many thanks go to these kind friends and family for supporting the creation of this book:

Jill Barancik, Shannon Brandt, Alden Brandt-Cannon, William Harrison Cannon, Myfanwy Collins, Wendell Wood Collins, Chris Davis, Henry Dean, Amber Dermont, Tony Duran, Bill Gau, Erick Gordon, Jennifer Harfeld, Sommer Hixson, Stephanie Hunt, Brian Huskey, Chuck Kelly, Erik Kraft, Graham Kraft, Juliette LaMontagne, Christina Lomax, Erin McColl, Collin Oberndorf, Michael O'Briant, Andrew Olsen, Kirsten Olsen, Stacy "Spott" Philpott, Karen Presnell, Nelly Reifler, Lynn Sally, Margaret Skinder, Logan Smith, Britt and Nicole Uzzell, Jeff and Frauke Weston, Elizabeth Wildman, Jake Wizner, and Kira Wizner.

For editorial guidance and encouragement, I am grateful to Lucas Church of the University of North Carolina Press; Joseph Parsons, formerly of UNC Press; Evan Kindley and Tom Lutz of the *Los Angeles Review of Books*; David Haglund of the *New Yorker*, formerly of *Slate*; Morgan Beatty of *People Holding*; Issa Clubb of the Criterion Collection; Michelle Brower; Robyn O'Neil; and Molly Minturn.

For vital support in an urgent time of need, my sincere thanks go to the Authors Guild, PEN America, MacDowell, and Millay Arts, and I genuinely apologize for talking about my divorce so much after dinner.

Thanks are due to my many pals and customers at stores #511 and #516. My gratitude extends especially to those who saved for me hundreds of the little green cards with the North Carolina map and state seal on them, found inside heavy boxes of sweet potatoes, and to my friends at the Dutchess Biercafe. Thanks for listening to me rattle on about Andy Griffith. You are all the best. "Deeee-licious."

Thanks go to all who spoke with me about this subject matter. There are too many to list, but I especially acknowledge Sam's friends. Thank you.

SELECTED BIBLIOGRAPHY

In researching this manuscript, I accumulated a mountain of information gleaned from numerous newspaper and magazine interviews, hours of video clips and interviews, in-person interviews, email and phone conversations, books, blog posts, social media messages, archives, gossip, and any other place searchable information is found. As I bounced around New England in the years after leaving New York City, a huge box of research came with me; I usually kept it under my desk, with one foot touching it at all times as I worked. On my computer and in the cloud, a folder titled "Looking for Andy Griffith" contains 1,983 items, which takes up about a gigabit of space, if that means anything now or in the future. Most of this information did not make it into the final manuscript but was nevertheless helpful.

Listed below are a few key sources for which I'm especially grateful.

Barthel, Joan. "How to Merchandise an Actor on TV." *New York Times Magazine*, October 25, 1970.

Burns, Ken, dir. *Jazz*. Produced by Ken Burns and Lynn Novick. Florentine Films, 2001.

Cole, Clay. *Sh-Boom! The Explosion of Rock 'n' Roll (1953–1968)*. Garden City, NY: Morgan James Publishing, 2009.

Crow, Jeffrey J. "Thomas Settle Jr., Reconstruction, and the Memory of the Civil War." *Journal of Southern History* 62, no. 4 (November 1996): 689–726.

Fimrite, Ron. "A Long Locomotive for Choo Choo." *Sports Illustrated*, October 15, 1973.

Freeman, Donald. "I Think I'm Gaining on Myself." *Saturday Evening Post*, January 24, 1964.

Huffman, Eddie. "Remembering Andy Griffith's 'What It Was, Was Football.'" *Greensboro News and Record*, August 27, 2017.

Koch, Frederich Henry, ed. *Carolina Folk-Plays*. New York: Henry Holt and Company, 1922.

Millstein, Gilbert. "Strange Chronicle of Andy Griffith." *New York Times Magazine*, June 2, 1957.

"Music: What It Is, Is Talk." *Time*, January 18, 1954.

Navy Department Communiques 1–300 and Pertinent Press Releases, December 10, 1941 to March 5, 1943. US Navy, Office of Public Relations. Washington, DC: Government Printing Office, 1943.

Private Screenings. Patricia Neal interviewed by Robert Osborne. TCM, 2004.

Rose, Frank. *The Agency: William Morris and the Hidden History of Show Business*. New York: Harper Business, 1995.

Trotter, William R. *Bushwhackers: The Civil War in North Carolina*. Vol. 2, *The Mountains*. Durham, NC: Blair, 1988.

The following sources were also a significant help:

Andy Griffith Papers, 1945–2005, Southern Historical Collection, Wilson Library, University of North Carolina at Chapel Hill

Archives of American Television, https://interviews.television academy.com/interviews

Atlanta Journal-Constitution

Daily Tar Heel

Hollywood Reporter

Los Angeles Times

Mount Airy News

NC Weekend (aired on UNC-TV)

North Carolina People with William Friday (aired on UNC-TV)

Variety

Virginian-Pilot